Endorsements for Don't Quit Your Church

I don't know any minister of the Gospel who has not contemplated walking away from it all. This book is a wise, careful word of encouragement that can be read through a time of stress, despair, crisis, or just on one of those Monday mornings when the adrenaline has crested and the task seems too big. Read it and don't give up.

—Russell D. Moore, Dean, The Southern Baptist Theological Seminary

Don't Quit is a solidly biblical and practical book that should be on every minister's bookshelf. Jeff Brown carefully and pastorally explores the blessings and difficulties of faithful gospel ministry. He addresses the challenges that cause us to ask, "Is it really worth it?" He then provides encouragement that will enable us to say, "Yes it is!"

—Daniel L. Akin, President, Southeastern Baptist Theological Seminary

Ministry is tough—something any ministry leader knows well. The problems associated with helping people, guiding projects, and struggling through personal issues comes with the territory. At times discouragement turns to despair and depression. The unthinkable—quitting a ministry assignment or even leaving the ministry—becomes a possibility. The ministry leader in despair needs the gentle guidance of truth before irreversible decisions are made. Jeff Brown's book provides just that guidance. What he has written is biblical, thoughtful, probing, and practical. Before you make a decision in despair to leave a ministry assignment, read this. It can't hurt. It might even save a ministry.

—Sam Simmons, Cofounder, Rockbridge Seminary

Many times I have prayed with those who are going through difficult times in ministry and wished I had a book to share with them. This book is simple and practical, written by one who understands the heart and calling of a pastor. The author encourages ministers to ask tough sacred questions that will guide us to the next step in the journey. The book is filled with hope.

—Daryl Eldridge, President and Cofounder,
Rockbridge Seminary

DON'T QUIT YOUR
CHURCH

DON'T QUIT YOUR
CHURCH

What to Know Before You Leave Your Present Ministry

JEFF BROWN

WIPF & STOCK · Eugene, Oregon

Wipf and Stock Publishers
199 W 8th Ave, Suite 3
Eugene, OR 97401

Don't Quit Your Church
What to Know Before You Leave Your Present Ministry
By Brown, Jeffrey D.
Copyright©2016 by Brown, Jeffrey D.
ISBN 13: 978-1-5326-3297-6
Publication date 5/17/2017
Previously published by Tate Publishing & Enterprises, LLC , 2016

This book is dedicated to my wife (Brea) and children (Dani, Linnea, and Colin) as well as pastors and their families everywhere who do the Lord's work each week.

> Upon this rock I will build My church; and the gates of Hades will not overpower it.
>
> —Jesus (Matthew 16:18b)

Contents

Introduction: Our Greatest Need—Questions and Answers?.. 11

Part 1: Asking Questions in Your Context

1. Is God Finished with Me Here? 17
2. What Does a Biblical Exit Look Like? 27

Part 2: Finding Answers in Ephesus

3. Ride Out the Difficult Times (Acts 20:17–19).................... 41
4. Be a Man of the Word (Acts 20:20–21, 26)........................ 59
5. Be Humble and Selfless (Acts 20:22–24) 71
6. Leave Things Better than You Found Them (Acts 20:28–32)... 81
7. Be a Colaborer (Acts 20:33–35) 89
8. Open Your Heart to Them (Acts 20:36–38) 99

Part 3: Strategies in Moving Forward

9. Heed Paul's Pastoral Advice (1 and 2 Timothy) 115
10. Pray Effectively for a Healthy Church............................... 125
11. Be Spirit-led in Your Ministry 141

12 Let the Profound Define You	151
Afterward: Our Reward	163
Endnotes	165

INTRODUCTION

Our Greatest Need—Questions and Answers?

No one wants to fail. This is especially true for ministers who feel both called and gifted to lead. Church ministry has both personal and eternal significance and perceived failure in this arena is always something that a pastor takes personally. Recovery from a perceived failure in the ministry is both complicated and difficult. Some ministers never recover—abandoning their calling altogether. Others either continue on in their current context in a limited capacity, or move on to a different church hoping for something better. Even so, neither the minister nor the church is ever the same.

Many authors/experts do their best to prevent such nightmares from taking place. Others hope to help pick up the pieces once a ministry has collapsed. Excellent resources can be found in both of these areas. However, rather than writing on the subjects of how to have a great ministry or giving advice on how to deal with failure in the ministry, this book chooses a different, much less-traveled path. *What you hold in your hand is a ministerial lifeline of sorts for those who feel the boat is sinking at a rapid pace and are considering when to "jump ship."* Most ministers have been or will be in this predicament; few have had biblical words of advice offered to them.

Hopefully, this book is what is needed most for church staffs who are disappointed by failure, ready to walk away and in desperate need of guidance. I pray that this will not just be another book, but that God will use it to give you clarity. Perhaps looking at things once again will be something that God can use to mend both the church and the pastor. Like success, failure can be something we have "earned" or something we have had handed to us. But a change of course—a decision of forgiveness, refocus, and renewal—is always an act of will. Fortunately, it is an option that God has made available if we are willing to make the right decisions.

When hope is running dry and failure seems all but certain, most ministers choose to put on a brave face. However, in such times, discernment is much more valuable than bravery. Preaching, teaching, and counseling ministries are fueled by biblical solutions to life's problems. For a leader, not knowing what is going on in one's own life can be quite frustrating and painful. However, the issue of ministerial doubt and struggle is found quite often throughout church history in both the Old and New Testaments. God is used to having His children stand in a cloud of confusion, battling doubt and literally fighting for air. He is more than ready to rescue and stand closer than ever before.

Ministers would much rather prefer to give answers than to ask questions. As a pastor and a professor who trains pastors, I challenge students and parishioners to realize that they have been given so many answers about doctrine, faith, and purpose without ever asking a single question. Although nice in some ways, this has robbed postmodern Christianity of the process of "treasure hunting" and the satisfaction of individually coming to conclusions. It has also made our decisions often more affected by feeling than thinking. In general, questions should at least equal answers if education is to be reflective and thoughtful. Although answers are much more enjoyable than questions, when questions are all that we have, they must be addressed clearly, concisely, and biblically.

For those who are definitely perplexed and in danger of despair, the process toward hope, clarity, and purpose makes answers mandatory. With this in mind, this book contains only two questions and ten answers! The questions are intended to be more personal, reflective, and hopefully spiritually therapeutic. The solutions are unapologetically biblical. The questions address the past and present. The answers are what move the struggling minister forward and come from questions I have asked, other ministers have asked me, and—most likely—ones that you have been asking for quite some time.

PART 1

Asking Questions in Your Context

1

Is God Finished with Me Here?

Questions about success and failure regarding the ministry have been far too subjective for far too long. Typically, the assessment of a ministry is based on effort and intention while very little space is given to question philosophy, methodology, faithfulness, and biblical soundness regarding one's service. Most mistakes in any given ministry are committed at the beginning and the end of a particular tenure, but the most serious one—and the most tempting—is leaving before it's time.

The differences between finishing a task and hastily walking away from a ministry have far too often lost distinction. As a result, excessive numbers of ministers have prematurely exited places of service to where they once felt genuinely called and from which they have never felt unmistakably called away. These decisions are often surrounded by emotions: anger, bitterness, personal doubt, etc. However, the only real reason to leave must be a spiritual one. If it is not, the problems only become more complicated for everyone. Although the Lord does move in mysterious ways, His calling to leave a place of ministry is equally as clear as His call to come. Unfortunately, few ministers enjoy such clarity at the end of their tenure.

There is a clear option to the tumultuous "endgame" that you may be considering. It is a plan that can battle these negative emotions and clear up God's calling to stay or to go. It sounds simple, perhaps obvious, but the one element that keeps more people in a difficult ministry besides calling is a clear understanding of *what* they were called to accomplish in a given context. These key elements of call and vision are the best anchors in tumultuous times. In reality, most ministers are not clear in regard to what they were supposed to accomplish when they were called to a church. However, the biblical reality remains that ministry has clearly defined objectives. Some are easy to measure and some are not. Even so, there is enough in Scripture to not only offer advice when it comes to exiting a current ministry but also to serve as a guide during the most difficult times.

The answer to this chapter's question must be addressed on two levels; the most basic question is, "Am I ready to become a statistic?" A deeper, more spiritual question asks, "Have I accomplished all that God sent me here to do?" This second and most profound question rarely receives attention in such a situation. Its aim is to know definitively if God is finished with your current ministry and context. Are there young believers He has for you to disciple, lost who are on the brink of conversion, a stubborn traditionalist who needs a bit more patience, ruffled feathers that need to be calmed, etc.? The minister may be finished with the church and the church finished with the minister, but is *God* finished with the work? That is the only question that should matter.

When God calls people away, they are typically not ready to go. Nor is the church ready to let them go. It is a time of surrender and submission to God's will. The only biblical "good-bye" is the one that God alone forces for the greater good of the Kingdom. Like all other decisions regarding calling, it is preceded with prayer, made in wisdom and discernment, and carried through in grace. However, few pastoral exits have anything in common with these concepts. Perhaps a time of pause, reflection, and evaluation is in order?

Am I Ready to Become a Statistic?

Church work for conservative evangelical ministers is a mixed bag to say the least. Often the same minister—using the same techniques, holding the same convictions, and implementing the same ministries—can and will find radically different results, depending on the context. Some pastorates are great, others unfortunately become nightmares. It seems that for every success story, there are many more instances that have only sad and seemingly empty conclusions. Many ministers have unfortunately called it quits and many churches have simply given up on their prospects for a bright future and instead are looking to limit the pain in their final years. Fewer qualified young men are currently entering the ministry.[1] Short tenures, boiling tempers, and hurt feelings describe many ministerial departures in conservative churches. Noticeably, the number of healthy churches and effective ministries are seriously lacking among American evangelicals.

There are at least three ways to end a ministry, and only one is biblically sound. The first two include either the church forcing an exit or the minister walking away before it is time. Even though most tenures end in the wrong way—with either the church or minister halting the relationship—there are those good-byes that are worth having and that speak volumes about the character of God Himself. The end of a ministry can indeed be a witness to a lost world. Unfortunately, in an individualistic world of entitlement, it is too often quite the opposite.

Churches decide that it is time to let ministers go for various reasons, some good and some bad. Although it is hard to know for sure what percentage of churches have forced resignations from their pastors, it seems that everyone knows of such a church. In a survey of nearly six hundred pastors, 91% knew of a pastor who had been forced to resign.[2] Although there is great diversity in the reason for the firings, some common themes emerge when the issue is examined closely. Although we would suppose that the church's grievance must be quite monumental to warrant a pastoral termination, often this is not the case. Rather than being accusations of infidelity, heresy, or other integrity issues, most forced exits are based around less pressing problems such as personality conflicts, styles of leadership, preferences in worship, unmet expectations, and conflicting visions. Usually the battle is fought between the minister and minority factions within the church.[3]

These forced resignations have residual effects. It seems that neither party is able to fully heal from such a painful experience. A significant number of ministers who are forced to leave the ministry drop out altogether while the churches they leave often seek to fill the vacancy quickly.[4] The feelings of bitterness, failure, and spiritual inadequacy that follow are often with both the congregation and the former pastor for quite some time. Even so, it is not simply the fault of the church and/or her members that ministries are not given the opportunity to see divine fruit. In fact, most early exits are not forced upon the pastor; they are rather seized by him.

Voluntary and willful resignations that are offered on the part of the minister continue to be a serious issue among our churches and are much more common than terminations forced by the church. The most common rationales for resigning deal with the church's unwillingness to change, the church's inability to compensate for an acceptable standard of living, or God's leading elsewhere.[5] The problem is really twofold. First, the pastor has lost hope in the church ever becoming what God expects; and second, he has lost confidence in himself to be able to lead the church to that place. To put it plainly, we ministers often choose to give up on God's plan, perhaps more for a lack of patience than anything else.

Voluntary, but impulsive departures often display the common aforementioned emotions of frustration, inadequacy, impatience, anger, and bitterness. These feelings of contention and lack of harmony between the pastor and the congregation have been referred to as the "dirty little secret" for conservative evangelicals.[6] Often a pastor's early exit is due to a lapse in recognizing the greater picture regarding the eternal nature of the ministry.

The question at hand remains quite simple, "Am I ready to become one of these awful statistics?" The decisions made during this time can and will define whether your ministry becomes a failure or a success. It will most likely help determine your legacy and the church's. Here are some sobering thoughts from a recent survey:

- 1,500 pastors across all denominations leave the ministry each month due to burnout, forced termination, moral failure, compassion fatigue, or marital difficulties.
- 80% of seminary and Bible school graduates who enter the ministry will leave the ministry within the first five years.
- 60% to 80% of those who enter the ministry will not still be in it ten years later.
- 89% of the pastors surveyed also considered leaving the ministry at one time. 57% said they would leave if they had a better place to go—including secular work.
- 50% of pastors are so discouraged they would leave the ministry if they could but have no other way of making a living.
- 77% of the pastors surveyed felt they did not have a good marriage!
- 70% of pastors constantly fight depression.
- Almost 40% of ministers polled said they have had an extramarital affair since beginning of their ministry.
- 38% of pastors said they were divorced or currently in a divorce process.
- 80% of pastors' wives wish their husbands would choose another profession.
- The majority of pastors' wives surveyed said that the most destructive event which has occurred in their marriage and family was the day they entered ministry.[7]

Perhaps we might be hopeful enough to believe that these are isolated numbers, but they are not. The vast majority of surveys tell the same sad story. Clearly, the most rewarding of callings often becomes the most painful. When this happens, many simply walk away—that is, if they have somewhere else to go.

It is quite obvious that pastoral tenures on the average are not nearly long enough to allow a church and minister to really get to know each other, let alone to develop a vision and plan of implementation for the future of the congregation. Consistently, the average tenure among churches where the congregation calls its own leadership is between two to four years. Other statistics in the past twenty years have leaned toward the two to three year range. Anecdotal evidence shows much longer tenures among pastors going into the ministry in the past two decades. Tenures of four to eight years seem to be more common. If it pans out, this is indeed a promising trend since it is quite clear that healthy churches demand a solid tenure. Unfortunately, a very small percentage of pastorates see a noteworthy legacy left behind in their absence. As a result, the minister, his family, and the church suffer.[8]

There is no way to know the exact percentage of clergy who give up or how many choose to work through their various struggles. However, it seems that many are quite clear in their calling but perhaps not sure of their context. While some do leave the ministry, churches do not close doors when this happens, and most ministers do not walk away from the ministry altogether. There are plenty of empty pulpits that need to be filled every Sunday morning. Some may say this is a sad statement about the downfall of Christianity in America. As an optimist, it says to me that we have not given up yet! This reality holds promise that can motivate those who are struggling.

Have I Accomplished All that God Sent Me Here to Do?

Subjectivity must be minimized in regard to ministerial success. After hearing dozens—if not hundreds—of stories of dysfunctional ministries and churches, everyone always attempts to "look on the bright side" by saying, "Although the tenure was only months long, God did a lot of things during that time," "It was a learning experience," or "The resignation, though sad, was best for everyone…" We have all heard or employed these inadequate excuses for walking away and giving up. In truth, it is quite difficult to find the positive about a ministry that was cut short before God said that it was time. It is a divorce, a broken fellowship, and many hurt children have been left disillusioned in the wake of these decisions.

There is only one way that a pastor should ever be able to justify leaving a ministry (aside from health issues or other life's challenges that rightly take his focus away) and that is with the knowledge that the mission has been accomplished and the objectives have been met. There is no doubt that a sizable amount of ministry is subjective. However, that element of objective, clearly defined goals are tools in God's hand to lend toward stability, clarity, and discernment and can give the church and the minister patience, vision, and hope. God can always change plans; however, that never implies that ministries should not have them.

More time should be spent on measurable goals. Clearly, it is hard to know exactly when someone is "healthy" or "mature" let alone an entire body of believers. However, there is much to ministry that is measurable and should be evaluated. We can measure new programs and ministries, volunteer involvement, stewardship, and zeal. As well, we as ministers can evaluate our attitude, commitment, and effectiveness in most every area of church service. Most pastors go into a church ministry with a list of things to do but not a list of things to get done. We preach, teach, counsel, evangelize, etc. This is just the way we "do church." These are the things we put on our resumes and the items that churches list in their pastoral search advertisements. Instead, we must also ask what was God hoping to accomplish through this partnership—and then we must abandon all things to achieve this goal!

Conclusion: Endurance as the Key

One consistent command throughout Scripture that serves as a unifying theme of God's expectation on His people is endurance. Jesus Himself tells us that it is those who endure to the end who will be saved (Matthew 24:13). He even rebuked His disciples for their lack of endurance when they were expected to watch and pray but instead fell asleep (Mark 14:37). Solomon warned his sons not to rest on their own understanding but to trust in God even during difficult times (Proverbs 3:5–8). Whether it is Abraham, Moses, a prophet, or disciple, endurance was expected, especially during difficult times. James promised that endurance produces hope and boldness (James 1:2–4). The same expectation and promise holds true today.

As we will see in chapter 9, Paul had much to say to pastors. However, there is one command pertinent to this discussion that Paul gives Pastor Timothy. Paul realized that Ephesus was not the easiest place to be a pastor. As well, he understood that Timothy most likely felt inexperienced and inadequate for what he was called to do. There was no doubt that false teachers were trying to take down the church theologically and Timothy spiritually. Without a doubt, Timothy was thinking about leaving his ministry there in the most difficult context. So Paul, as a father in the faith, commands Timothy to do something that would have taken great discernment, determination, and discipline. He instructed him to "stay on in Ephesus" (1 Timothy 1:3). For many, it is a verse that is passed in order to get to rest of the letter. However, for ministers in a "sinking ship," this must become an anthem! This book will exhort you, as Paul exhorted Timothy, to stay on in your current ministry!

This command assumes several realities. First, God is still working. Second, there is still hope for a successful ministry. Third, you have faith that God can change people (including you), and finally, that nothing worth having comes easily. Struggling ministers *must* assume a posture of staying when difficulty strikes. It is indeed the biblical response. There has to be an assumption of ministerial longevity in all matters. It is not over until God says it is! It is wise to assume that in most situations God would make such information quite clear. Stay put until you know for sure.

2

What Does a Biblical Exit Look Like?

Everyone involved in the ministry, especially the pastoral ministry, is clear on one fact: working with a community of believers is a very complex endeavor. This should be no surprise to anyone since Scripture refers to the Gospel as a mystery, humanity as both extremely desperate and hugely prideful, the followers of Christ as sheep, church leaders as slaves, our Savior as a suffering servant, and the enemy as a deceptive wolf! No doubt, this type of situation is the very stuff that complexity is made of! Even with the guidance of Scripture and the Holy Spirit, virtually every aspect of living in God's Kingdom is difficult to grasp fully. Pastoral ministry is no exception since it is the most profound and important office of human responsibility in existence.

Since the genuine fruits of pastoral ministry do indeed take a great amount of time to harvest, anything that can be done to enhance a tenure—and perhaps prolong it—is worthy of attention. The more time that we spend on the field, the greater chance there is for a bountiful harvest. A comprehensive understanding of the ministry is unattainable. Nonetheless, God does desire to see significant tenures that are effective, purposeful, and growing stronger each year.

In order to define success in church ministry, God gave some basic guidelines throughout Scripture. From the foundation of Mosaic Law to the ministry of Christ, Pentecost, and beyond, we find a definition of ministerial success in methodology, philosophy, and mission. The most specific description is found in Paul's ministry to the Ephesians. In it we find a comprehensive approach of God's will for the everyday life of church ministry. From the Pauline approach, spiritual success *can* be defined and prescribed. In order to have a successful tenure, you must earn the right to be called away. Contrary to popular opinion and practice, there is no doubt that a minister can objectively know when a ministry is truly completed (rather than halted). This fact speaks volumes regarding how ministers can stay on track when things are difficult. When the exit is as sure of a call as the entrance, the end is justified, not just accepted.

The Means that Justifies the End

The act of leading and/or shepherding a congregation is both a science and an art.[10] Accepting this truth is essential for a pastor's and church's mental and spiritual health. Both parties rely on a combination of knowledge and intuition in making decisions. These decisions range from calling a pastor and in moving forward with the overall vision. It is amazing how often this inexact science works! However, it does not find much success at the end of one's tenure. Perhaps exiting one's church should require more science and less art.

The conclusion that it is time to leave must come only through intense scrutiny, research, communication, fasting, and prayer. This decision is far too important to be a product of emotion, feeling, or intuition without clear divine knowledge.

We see in Scripture that the decision for leaving a place of ministry was a titanic struggle for Paul. Knowing what was next and where to go was much more than a personal desire for him. The apostle considered leaving Ephesus and actually desired to go to Corinth, a church with comparable needs. However, he wrote the Corinthian church in 1 Corinthians 16:8–9 about his decision to stay in Ephesus, "But I will remain in Ephesus until Pentecost; for a wide door for effective service has opened to me, and there are many adversaries." His exit was as calculated as his entrance had been. It was not determined by the struggles of the current context nor his desire to do other works.

The question then is simple. How does one truly, objectively know that it is time to leave a given ministry? How can such an emotional situation be decided in an objective manner where the preacher and the congregation are both in agreement that it is time to say good-bye? The definitive evaluation of a successful ministry, and therefore whether or not one is truly finished at a church, can be found in Acts 20 in the apostle's farewell speech to the Ephesians' elders/pastors[11] where he not only felt it was time to move on but also knew it conclusively.

The problem of ineffective pastoral tenure can be aided by a real "job description," and one is found through a study of this passage which also served as a sort of training session for the Ephesians' pastors.[12] For the contemporary problem of forced resignations, temper tantrums, hurt feelings, early retirements, and abrupt resignations, Paul's final words to the Ephesians' elders offer a level of objectivity to truly determine whether *God* is ready to move on or not.

It is worth repeating, like the beginning, the ending of a ministry must be ordained by God and the right to say good-bye must be earned and confirmed by a hope for future church growth, consent by the proper authorities, and an undeniable inner peace. The Miletus speech stands alone in its contribution to every ministry and every minister. It is indeed unequaled in all of Scripture.[13]

> From Miletus he sent to Ephesus and called to him the elders of the church. And when they had come to him, he said to them, 'You yourselves know, from the first day that I set foot in Asia, how I was with you the whole time, serving the Lord with all humility and with tears and with trials which came

upon me through the plots of the Jews; how I did not shrink from declaring to you anything that was profitable, and teaching you publicly and from house to house, solemnly testifying to both Jews and Greeks of repentance toward God and faith in our Lord Jesus Christ. And now, behold, bound in spirit, I am on my way to Jerusalem, not knowing what will happen to me there, except that the Holy Spirit solemnly testifies to me in every city, saying that bonds and afflictions await me. But I do not consider my life of any account as dear to myself, so that I may finish my course and the ministry which I received from the Lord Jesus, to testify solemnly of the gospel of the grace of God. And now, behold, I know that all of you, among whom I went about preaching the kingdom, will no longer see my face. Therefore, I testify to you this day that I am innocent of the blood of all men. For I did not shrink from declaring to you the whole purpose of God. Be on guard for yourselves and for all the flock, among which the Holy Spirit has made you overseers, to shepherd the church of God which He purchased with His own blood. I know that after my departure savage wolves will come in among you, not sparing the flock; and from among your own selves men will arise, speaking perverse things, to draw away the disciples after them. Therefore be on the alert, remembering that night and day for a period of three years I did not cease to admonish each one with tears. And now I commend you to God and to the word of His grace, which is able to build you up and to give you the inheritance among all those who are sanctified. I have coveted no one's silver or gold or clothes. You yourselves know that these hands ministered to my own needs and to the men who were with me. In everything I showed you that by working hard in this manner you must help the weak and remember the words of the Lord Jesus, that He Himself said, 'It is more blessed to give than to receive.' " When he had said these things, he knelt down and prayed with them all. And they began to weep aloud and embraced Paul, and repeatedly kissed him, grieving especially over the word which he had spoken, that they would not see his face again. And they were accompanying him to the ship. (Acts 20:17–38)

By understanding the different elements of what Paul considered a standard for ministry, both a methodology and philosophy of ministry can be developed that will enable one to have biblically defined and Spirit-empowered tenure. Notably, it is Paul's longest speech and the only speech recorded that the apostle delivered to Christians.[14]

The details of this passage are paramount for our understanding of what ministry is supposed to be and has been given its place among the great "farewells" of Scripture.[15] The speech itself makes nearly twenty claims alluding to the past, the present, and the future. About half reflect what he did among them, nine depending on how it is broken down, one general statement is a testimony to his future calling (vv. 22–24), and five warnings are particularly offered to the overseers with whom he is speaking.

These various elements of the speech can be divided under three particular headings. Each one offers the evidence that Paul brings forth to his fellow ministers to make the case that the job was finished and done in a biblical manner. Paul claims that he was faithful, his work among them was a success, and that they were able to handle whatever came their way.

Hope in the Church's Future

In these final words we can see an apostle who was clear about what he was called to do among them, confident in what he had attempted, and assured that the work would continue in his absence. One of the basic principles of ministry is to leave the church better than it was when the ministry began. Church ministry is holy and spiritual success can indeed happen on so many levels if we remember that a job is finished when God, congregation, and minister are all satisfied with the work that God had mercifully done in their given context. It is only then that God will convince *both* parties that they are ready to part ways. When God is orchestrating an exit, the future holds no doubts, questions, or regrets, only fondness, appreciation, and hope.

Consent by the Proper Authorities

Not only was Paul confident that the future bode well for the church, he was also certain that his departure was appropriate because he had recognized and submitted to the three authorities that were in place: God, his own conscience, and the church. He states in his farewell that his hands were clean before God,[16] he was self-assured that he had accomplished what he was called to do. As well, we see that the congregation was convinced that Paul had given it his all as well. These are the three "authorities" to which all ministers must answer.

Ultimately, God remains the final and ultimate authority. However, He speaks to both the minister's conscience and the congregation's discernment to make His will known. If a minister wishes to end or fundamentally change a divinely ordained relationship, it will not simply be a personal conviction or preference. Divine confirmation will be given for such a serious decision, and a minister should be certain to wait for such guidance.

An Undeniable Inner Peace

Paul's ministerial effort in Ephesus brought about a very rare commodity among Christian ministers, a genuine peace about the past and the future. Paul was a deep thinker. Throughout the New Testament, Paul demonstrates his intellectual approach to ministry. Consider the number of times that the apostle says, "I am persuaded" or "I am convinced." Relocation was a spiritual, emotional, and intellectual endeavor. God used many things to move His apostle from one place to the next. Paul particularly had been guided to relocate through: visions, revelations from the Lord, encouragements by others, and pleas for help. He would not talk himself out of staying on at a church. In fact, he would not move until he *knew* that he was called to go. For him, leaving Ephesus needed ultimate clarity. Paul believed, after a serious evaluation, that divine victory had been granted in Ephesus. Now all he had to do was convince the Ephesians' elders of the same. The Miletus speech can enable us to have peace of mind when it comes to exiting a ministry. If we have done the work that Paul did, we can *know* that there is nothing left for God to do through us at a particular place of service. In this speech we see the particulars of what a successful and complete ministry looks like.

Preparing for the End of the Tunnel

For any minister who has just relocated to a new ministry, leaving is not something that sounds particularly enticing. So many boxes are yet to be unpacked, so much excitement is still alive, and so many butterflies are still floating around in various stomachs. However, we must not wait very long before creating an exit strategy that includes what they would define as success in that particular place of service. The reasons for this are manifold and are based firmly in the reality that all ministries will eventually come to an end.

An early formation of an exit strategy is needed to give sharpened focus to the minister regarding his task and to the church to understand the vital role that each member must play. Once we seriously consider what it is that God has called us to achieve in a given context, we have basically painted ourselves in a corner and cannot move until a certain amount of time passes. Spiritual success takes time, and faithfulness and patience go hand in hand. The compiling of priorities, specific goals, and desired accomplishments will do much to add both quality and quantity to the pastoral tenure of ministers. Sharing this vision with those in the church is a positive thing. It creates credibility, allows accountability, builds trust and—most importantly—unity as the body attempts to reach new heights together.

A clear understanding of the task will certainly lead to a stronger relationship between the minister and the Savior. Such a reality will humble and perhaps awaken us to the true calling of the King. The arrival at such important knowledge will require that much prayer, and reflection is mingled with a genuine attempt to understand the vision of the congregation itself. The experience will do much to grow the pastor into a mature Christian, lacking nothing and carrying wisdom beyond his years.

A biblical exit strategy that is formed early on in your ministry will allow for an all-too-often neglected element of prayer, meditation, and reflection. Ministers always speak humbly about not knowing the will of God, but often they behave as if they understand every detail. Having a concrete list of what should be done will cause serious evaluation early on, keep ministers focused for longer, hold them stationary when other temptations to leave may arrive, and will give them clear and objective confirmation that it is indeed time to move on once the goals have been reached.

Writing a farewell speech that incorporates the elements of Paul's farewell to the Ephesians will make submission to God's authority mandatory. It will minimize personal opinion and preconceived notions. As well, it will result in more clarity and efficiency. The reality is that churches change and ministers change. Being able to adapt to change is good. A plan can always be adjusted and should always be willing to bend to the divine guidance of the moment. Nevertheless, a plan cannot be dictated by struggles and temptations nor should it be developed as one goes along. When each ministry, each committee, and each sermon/lesson and service has a purpose before it and a goal in mind, God's people will soon understand why some things must be done, some are simply permissible and others are outside of the scope and purpose of the church.

If a minister in contemporary America is to have an exit from a ministry that is biblical in spirit, it must be founded on a ministry that was biblically consistent as well. Today, far too many models are based on "what worked for pastor 'so and so'" and not what is defined in Scripture. With the number of firings and forced resignations being historically higher in recent years and the number of ministers willing to enter the ministry being decisively lower, healthy tenures that begin and end with faith, hope, and love are more imperative than ever. However, only the minister who will depend on biblical definitions, build on a biblical foundation and will measure success only through a biblically objective lens will be allowed such a glorious farewell as Paul was granted.

Without a doubt, Paul did not simply happen to do the right things, he was predisposed to excellence. He knew what he wanted to accomplish for Christ and by the grace of God, he did it! Ministers of today must develop a strategy that seeks to honor God's call, the people's genuine needs, and their own clear consciences. This is truly the heart of a healthy, functional success.

Leaving a Legacy in Our Time

Whether it was Ephesus or another city, Paul was determined to leave the congregation stronger than he found it. Whether he planted the church, felt compelled to write a letter, taught against heresy or simply preached in her midst, Paul committed to do things right. Everything that he accomplished and reported in these final words to the Ephesians was intentional. All ministers are called to be great leaders. Paul was a great leader because he was called to greatness and remained determined under all circumstances to fulfill Christ's expectation of him. He was beyond accusation because that was the ministry that he desired to have and was committed to conduct. The apostle was able to say good-bye with a clear conscience because he had indeed left the church in better shape than he had found it, knew that they were mature, and had confidence that they would be able to stand any test that would come their way (vv. 28–32).

It would be interesting to know how many pastors would have similar faith in their congregation to continue in health after their tenure ended. Nothing is guaranteed after a minister leaves, but only the right kind of ministry can produce the spiritually minded church that will continue a move in a godly direction. These priorities of the Pauline ministry are indeed the stuff of which legacies are built. Unfortunately, far too few churches/ministers display this Pauline expertise in ministry. The writing is on the wall, if one does not plan for the future, the future will devour them.

At its basic level, the idea of an early construction of a farewell speech begs the question of what the church will look like after a particular ministry ends. Whether the end is planned or not, what would the church do in the pastor's absence? The obvious hope for all ministers would be for the church to thrive, move forward, and quickly find new leadership. Unfortunately, far too many pastors have not left such an option for their prior tenure because they have failed as faithful stewards.[17]

The development of healthy congregations will take time, sacrifice, and diligence. Fortunately for us, success is not defined in numbers or efficiency by the world's standards. For ministers, it deals with faithfulness: Isaiah's faithfulness to preach to hardened hearts, Ezekiel's faithfulness to warn unconcerned citizens, Amos's faithfulness to cry out to comfortable people of wealth, and Jesus's perfect faithfulness to offer a light that His own people would try to snuff out. Notice, Paul did not claim victory. He did not boast of the growth of the church during his tenure. He did not brag of the baptisms or the recognition he received from associations or conventions. He simply stated with passion that he did the best he could and he was proud of his effort and extremely proud of them. No other good-bye could prove more profound than this.

Conclusion: The Called-On Call

A myriad of ministers promise pulpit committees that their intention is to stay at the prospective congregation for an indefinite amount of time. Yet, few of those pastors last over three to four years. Some exits are due to unbiblical reasons, others legitimately have God's hand on them. Knowing that God is in control of our "coming in and going out" should spur us to a more intense ministry. Our Commander is indeed mysterious and only informs us on a need-to-know basis. With all of this in mind, the ministry of the future must happen now. The end result must become our present priority.

Both ministers and churches must commit to serve with confidence rather than comfort and should entertain the reality that any Sunday could be the last opportunity that they hold to make a critical difference where they currently find themselves. What will the farewell look like? That is up to us as Christian ministers. What should it look like? It should look like Christ, confident and yet humble, who was a faithful servant and yet an inspiring leader, one who had given everything and was not ashamed to ask others to do the same. Perhaps your next good-bye could be something special; perhaps it could historically parallel Paul's.

> When he had said these things, he knelt down and prayed with them all. And they began to weep aloud and embraced Paul, and repeatedly kissed him, grieving especially over the word which he had spoken, that they would not see his face again. And they were accompanying him to the ship. (Acts 20:36–38)

When the inevitable time does arrive, such a scene can and will be possible if a solid effort has been made on behalf of God and His people. It can happen when the minister knows that nothing but the best has been offered. Surely, our Lord desires all ministries to end in a time of reflection, confidence, and closure. Even so, the reality of such an exit depends upon each minister and each congregation specifically. If the biblical mandate is followed, this dream will become a reality and indeed, the gates of hell itself will be unable to stop it.

PART 2

Finding Answers in Ephesus

3

Ride Out the Difficult Times (Acts 20:17–19)

Introduction: The Dreaded Meeting

He knew deep within himself that there was something empty about that particular day. He could not have anticipated the depth of the agony, and even after experiencing it, he still would not be able to fathom or completely explain it. He could see the looks on their faces even before they arrived. His heart was heavy and his mind weary. There were many things he could not predict about the fast-approaching meeting. However, he knew beyond any doubt how they would react; he was able to anticipate every word they would speak. There was no question that his heart was going to be shattered. He was walking into pain itself, and it was too late to turn back.

It wouldn't hurt so badly if he hadn't gotten so close to them. If only such an encounter was to be had with simple acquaintances, nominal "friends," or—even better—total strangers. But such a luxury was not to be afforded him. They were his once-fellow ministers, his close friends, his confidants, prayer partners, and covisionaries. At one time they were his greatest encouragers. Now their words would cut like knives, their reactions would utterly crush him, and his spirit would be tempted to a level that was formerly unknown. They were on their way. Decisions had been made, hearts had been convinced, and minds had been persuaded. Nothing now could change the future; nothing could be done, except for saying good-bye.

Something that was so special and so dear was now over. While his mind was set and solid, the rest of his being offered him no such clarity. His heart was uneasy and his emotions were running wild. The only thing he knew for sure was that the opportunity for ministry had come and gone. He had taught them everything he could and nothing more could be done at this point. The final task would be to pick up the pieces and leave. Indeed, that would be the only thing left to do.

Do Ministers Get a Happy Ending?

Much like a happy ending in marriage, the promise of bliss in ministry is often quite elusive these days. Ministry is much more often described as painful, challenging, sacrificial, and heartbreaking. The apostle Paul did not dispute these words. A quick glance at his various ministries makes this reality quite clear; he became angry with the Galatians to the point that he personally insulted them, his utter disappointment with the Corinthians justified a serious rebuke for their tolerance of blatant sin within the church body, his strong challenge of the Roman belief that "sin might make grace even stronger" demonstrated a clear frustration with their ignorance. It was not just churches that Paul struggled with, it was also people. He mentioned those spreading the Gospel as an attempt to take advantage of his imprisonment (Philippians 1), and he was forced to rebuke even Peter for promoting an attitude of segregation between Jews and Gentiles (Galatians 2). What we receive from Paul is a realistic understanding of ministry, one of the highest highs and the lowest lows.

Paul understood the enigmatic nature of the ministry and the minister's calling better than anyone. We can see this clearly in the two contrasting descriptions below found in the first Corinthian letter. The church at Corinth was challenging his authority, and he employed these portrayals to give the church an "insider's look" into the life and calling of a minister. One is sobering, the other encouraging. To understand ministry, there has to be a realization of both the disappointments and joys of the call. First, we start with the more realistic imagery of the call.

> Therefore, since we have this ministry, as we received mercy, we do not lose heart…For we do not preach ourselves but Christ Jesus as Lord, and ourselves as your bond-servants for Jesus' sake…But we have this treasure in earthen vessels, so that the surpassing greatness of the power will be of God and not from ourselves; we are afflicted in every way, but not crushed; perplexed, but not despairing; persecuted, but not forsaken; struck down, but not destroyed; always carrying about in the body the dying of Jesus, so that the life of Jesus also may be manifested in our body. For we who live are constantly being delivered over to death for Jesus' sake, so that the life of Jesus also may be manifested in our mortal flesh. So death works in us, but life in you. But having the same spirit of faith, according to what is written, 'I believed, therefore I spoke,' we also believe, therefore we also speak, knowing that He who raised the Lord Jesus will raise us also with Jesus and will present us with you. For all things are for your sakes, so that the grace which is spreading to more and more people may cause the giving of thanks to abound to the glory of God. Therefore we do not lose heart, but though our outer man is decaying, yet our inner man is being renewed day by day. For momentary, light affliction is producing for us an eternal weight of glory far beyond all comparison, while we look not at the things which are seen, but at the things which are not seen; for the things which are seen are temporal, but the things which are not seen are eternal. (2 Corinthians 4:1–18)

Looking at this sobering description of the minister, it seems that Paul is taking a long hard look at the difficulty of being in the ministry while at the same time balancing its eternal significance and divine foundation. At times ministry is trying and nearly beyond comprehension. However, for Paul, it was what it was—a difficult calling, but a calling nonetheless. It is absolutely essential that the heart of Paul's motivation is not missed by those struggling through their own ministry. What is it that keeps a minister going in difficult times?

> But having the same spirit of faith, according to what is written, 'I believed, therefore I spoke', we also believe, therefore we also speak, knowing that He who raised the Lord Jesus will raise us also with Jesus and will present us with you. For all things are for your sakes, so that the grace which is spreading to more and more people may cause the giving of thanks to abound to the glory of God. Therefore we do not lose heart... (2 Corinthians 4:13–18)

The foundational motivation of the ministry is nothing more than the ministry itself; the message, the people, the purpose, and ultimately the One doing the calling. All that the minister needs is clarity and self-discipline. Consider these key thoughts from D. Martyn Lloyd-Jones's classic work, *Spiritual Depression*.

> If we are unhappy and depressed Christians it is more than likely that it is all due to that lack of discipline. Let us therefore be up and doing, and giving all diligence, let us supplement our faith and not be afraid. Let us get our ideas clear and then put them to practice and supplement our faith with this vigor, with this knowledge, with this temperance, with this patience, godliness, brotherly kindness and love.[18]

The reward of your ministry is not success in ministry, but the peace of doing what you are called to do, and the perfect contentment of a being in the middle of God's will. Using Paul's logic, as it was revealed through Christ, success is found in faithfulness, not trophies, plaques, awards, positions, or even in personal satisfaction.

Dealing with Reality

We are inundated with the thought that if we keep moving in the right direction and with the right attitude, things will eventually turn around. Although this is a good basic strategy, it is not a prophecy-awaiting fulfillment. Much like broken relationships throughout our context, the ministerial relationship is ended because of unrealistic expectations. A brief look at the *Parable of the Talents* gives a more realistic view of the expectations of those who are called to follow Christ.

This parable is a familiar story told by Christ to make a point about being held accountable for what God has given us as individuals. It is very straightforward, but teaches us many important keys to being successful in service in the eyes of God. In the all-important context, this parable is preceded by the *Parable of the Ten Virgins*, encouraging preparedness for Christ's return and is followed by a teaching about the Second Coming itself. Clearly, this parable has eschatological implications. In that light, consider how eternally significant its words are.

> For it (the Kingdom of Heaven) is just like a man about to go on a journey, who called his own slaves and entrusted his possessions to them. To one he gave five talents, to another, two, and to another, one, each *according to his own ability*; and he went on his journey. Immediately the one who had received the five talents went and traded with them, and gained five more talents. In the same manner the one who had received the two talents gained two more. But he who received the one talent went away, and dug a hole in the ground and hid his master's money. Now after a long time the master of those slaves came and settled accounts with them. The one who had received the five talents came up and brought five more talents, saying, 'Master, you entrusted

five talents to me. See, I have gained five more talents.' His master said to him, 'Well done, good and faithful slave. You were faithful with a few things, I will put you in charge of many things; enter into the joy of your master.' Also the one who had received the two talents came up and said, 'Master, you entrusted two talents to me. See, I have gained two more talents.' His master said to him, 'Well done, good and faithful slave. You were faithful with a few things, I will put you in charge of many things; enter into the joy of your master.' And the one also who had received the one talent came up and said, 'Master, I knew you to be a hard man, reaping where you did not sow and gathering where you scattered no seed. And I was afraid, and went away and hid your talent in the ground. See, you have what is yours.' But his master answered and said to him, 'You wicked, lazy slave, you knew that I reap where I did not sow and gather where I scattered no seed. Then you ought to have put my money in the bank, and on my arrival I would have received my money back with interest. Therefore take away the talent from him, and give it to the one who has the ten talents. For to everyone who has, more shall be given, and he will have an abundance; but from the one who does not have, even what he does have shall be taken away. Throw out the worthless slave into the outer darkness; in that place there will be weeping and gnashing of teeth.' (Matthew 25:14–30)

The story is indeed full of important imagery and insight. At the end of time, accountability is something that all people will have to give for their lives. Ministers (teachers) will have even more to answer for (James 3:1). Note the key truths that can be drawn from this parable.

- All of those receiving money were slaves and unworthy of handling the master's funds.
- They were given an amount of money according to their abilities, not out of any special preference on behalf of, or relationship with the master.

- All three lived up to expectation whether it was high or low.
- The ones who doubled their original "talent" were given the same accolades even though they produced a different amount for the master.
- The one who did not reproduce was rebuked and removed.

Now, it is essential that one understands the differences between the two types of slaves, the faithful and good ones and the evil and lazy ones!

- The good slaves got busy immediately once the master left while the evil slave did not demonstrate any willingness to work for the master.
- The faithful slaves produced, and the evil one did not.
- The good servants were eager to meet their master while the wicked slave was not.
- The faithful servants willingly gave all the earnings to the master without question, it was always his money and not theirs.
- These faithful slaves were given the "joy of the master," which was much more than they had earned the master.
- The wicked slave blamed the master and claimed fear while the master called it laziness.
- The wicked servant lost everything and stood condemned.

Although we may not be quite comfortable with it, it is clear that faithful slaves produce fruit for the master. Those who make excuses because of their inadequacies or their "fear" of God reveal that they do not understand the heart of the master—neither his power nor his mercy.

I know that I'm not alone as either a pastor or a teacher when I say that I desire a "happy ending" for my ministry as well as the ministries of my students. Unfortunately, I must confess that it is most often up to us. While numbers and statistics may betray us, faithfulness will be the quality and characteristic by which we are judged. Many less-educated, less-qualified, and less-gifted ministers have done much more in more difficult circumstances. Read about them, study them, and note their attitudes, their convictions, and their utterly desperate dependence on the Lord. We read of them in Hebrews 11, we also note their stories in both church history and world history. They were crucified upside down. They were abandoned by their families, burned at the stake, beaten to death, exposed to intolerable cruelty toward their wives and children. They were shamed, humiliated and despised. They did not have a record book of baptisms to show Jesus when they died, nor nice plans on a new building they envisioned and raised funds for (not that these are not sufficient offerings). What they had to present before the Master is what every good servant throughout history has had to offer, and that is faithfulness.

Do you feel overwhelmed by such a "great cloud of witnesses"? I know I do. So, we have something in common with the writer of Hebrews and every other humble slave of the Kingdom. You may have only been given one talent. It may not sound like much, but scholars believe that one talent was about fifteen years of wages! Sure, it is less than thirty years of wages or seventy-five years of wages, but it is still plenty to work with!

When you feel that your contribution is small and that your task is minimal, consider these grand words of wisdom from one pastor to another. "I know the vanity of your heart, and that you will feel mortified that your congregation is very small, in comparison with those of your brethren around you; but assure yourself on the word of an old man, that when you come to give an account of them to the Lord Christ, at his judgment-seat, you will think you have had enough."[19] If you have been called, then you have been equipped. Even while being equipped as a minister, you still are being sanctified as a Christian. Your journey is more complex than others. While being called toward growth, you are expected to demonstrate humility. While having an expectation that you know most, if not all of the answers, you are called to be teachable. Whatever you have in front of you, those you have around you, and whatever God has done inside of you, this is your talent. The good news is that this is all you have to be faithful with!

Bitterness: Bitterness is among the English language's most nasty words. Just the sound of it makes people cringe. In layman's terms, it is a sour reaction to something that has not set right with an individual. It could be abuse, loss, grief, failure, betrayal, and the like. What it further implies is that this is an ongoing emotion that one cannot let go. In the ministry, it can be directed toward an individual or group, toward an event, a policy, a decision, or even toward God Himself. This happened many times in Scripture. Among the most memorable expressions of bitterness comes from the prophet Jonah who was bitter with God regarding Nineveh's revival. In the final lines of the book, God gives Jonah some shade and takes it away overnight. In his bitterness, Jonah wished to die! God would not answer Jonah's desperate prayer but instead used it as an example of God's love for Jonah's enemy. God has a right to be patient with evil men, and He has the right to expect the same from His servants.

Job was clearly bitter toward his situation, his friends, his wife, and God's silence. "I loathe my own life; I will give full vent to my complaint; I will speak in the bitterness of my soul" (Job 10:1). When he spoke such words, his friends would become even more accusatory, "whoever perished because they were righteous?" (Job 4:7), they would ask. Even in the midst of his darkest hour, God would not answer in Job's time.

Jeremiah wrote an entire Lamentation about his bitterness. Three times in chapter 3, he speaks of the bitterness that God has allowed upon him and the nation. A prophet who was already oversensitive—a weeper at heart—was the one chosen before his own conception to be a prophet for the Lord. He had a message of pain, sorrow, and future bondage based on Israel's past sins. The people's inability to hear wisdom and reply with sincerity and repentance was bad enough. However, the nation took it a step further and turned on Jeremiah personally. They rejected him for a false prophet (Jeremiah 18), locked him in stocks (Jeremiah 19), and called him names ("Terror on Every Side" in Jeremiah 20). No wonder he was bitter! God had called him to a life of pain without consulting him. He gave the prophet a horrible message of gloom, and He would not let him quit or walk away!

After the greatest discussion of faith and what faithful people look like, Hebrews 12:15 states, "See to it that no one comes short of the grace of God; that no root of bitterness springing up causes trouble, and by it may be defiled..." Bitterness should be understood as a natural response to what has happened in troubling situations. However, it cannot be seen as a biblical option. Ministers are especially commanded to resist it because of the "trouble" it will cause and the "defilement" that it can possibly bring about within the pastor's family and church.

Before moving on, it is important to briefly contextualize the outcome of our bitter friends! Jonah, although not happy, admitted that he knew God was so compassionate that Nineveh had a chance. He realized that same compassion had been lent to him. Although not the "ever after" ending that many would hope for, Jonah does at least acknowledge the root cause of his bitterness, he hated the fact that God loved his enemy! He was wrong to hate Nineveh, and he was also wrong to be bitter toward God for loving them. After God showed up to rebuke Job's "encroachment" on divine territory, Job was able to see God "with his own eyes" and repented of his bitterness. Jeremiah's melancholy nature did not move him away from his God, but rather kept him purposeful in his pursuit of truth. In the midst of his pain, he stated the profoundly powerful words, "The steadfast love of the Lord never ceases, His mercies never fail, they are new every morning. Great is your faithfulness!" Clearly, bitterness does not have to be the final stop in one's life or situation. If God is sought, He will be found (Jeremiah 29:13).

God has the ability to take away all bitterness if He is allowed to do so.

Anger: "He who is slow to anger has great understanding, but he who is quick-tempered exalts folly" (Solomon, Proverbs 14:29). Anger is perhaps the minister's worst enemy. Many ministries are thwarted, ended prematurely, or destroyed due to anger, one of the traditional "original sins" and one of the many fruits of the flesh mentioned in Galatians 5. It seems nearly everyone in the Bible became angry at one time or another, including God! Some were angry for selfish reasons like Cain, and others were quite justified in their anger like David who was insulted by Goliath's blasphemy.[20] Unfortunately, it seems that very little "righteous indignation" takes place anymore and yet many ministers want to claim their anger as a defense of God. If it's any consolation, the angry minister has much company including perhaps the most recognized and influential leader of world history, Moses. The story below gives us great insight into the issue at hand.

> Then the sons of Israel, the whole congregation, came to the wilderness of Zin in the first month; and the people stayed at Kadesh. Now Miriam died there and was buried there. There was no water for the congregation, and they assembled themselves against Moses and Aaron. The people thus contended with Moses and spoke, saying, 'If only we had perished when our brothers perished before the lord! Why then have you brought the lord's assembly into this wilderness, for us and our beasts to die here ...' Then Moses and Aaron came in from the presence of the assembly to the doorway of the tent of meeting and fell on their faces. Then the glory of the lord appeared to them; and the lord spoke to Moses, saying, 'Take the rod; and you and your brother Aaron assemble the congregation and speak to the rock before their eyes, that it may yield its water ...' So Moses took the rod from before the lord, just as He had commanded him; and Moses and Aaron gathered the assembly before the rock. And he said to them, 'Listen now, you rebels; shall we bring forth water for you out of this rock?' Then Moses

lifted up his hand and struck the rock twice with his rod; and water came forth abundantly, and the congregation and their beasts drank. But the lord said to Moses and Aaron, 'Because you have not believed Me, to treat Me as holy in the sight of the sons of Israel, therefore you shall not bring this assembly into the land which I have given them …' Then the lord spoke to Moses and Aaron…'Aaron will be gathered to his people; for he shall not enter the land which I have given to the sons of Israel, because you rebelled against My command at the waters of Meribah.' (Numbers 20:1–24)

It was Moses's and Aaron's anger that kept them personally from entering into the promised land. God said speak to the rock and Moses instead struck it twice and instead spoke to the congregation with scathing words of rebuke. Some might consider this a slipup, God considered it "disbelief" and "an insult to His holiness." This was indeed a high cost for a seemingly minor human error. Numbers 20 shows us clearly that God does not approve of "fit-throwing" ministers. If Moses could not get away with it, we should not expect to either. We cannot misrepresent God to His people; it will not go unpunished.

What we learn from Moses is that God expects us to hold it together in all situations. Moses had just lost his sister and was not dealing with the accusations of God's people regarding something he had no control over. This was the same Moses and the same congregation that Moses had interceded for on several occasions. Even so, God wanted the people to see His providence, mercy, and love, not Moses's tantrum. He does not tolerate ministers who cannot control their tempers.

The good news, I suppose, is that we are not alone in this struggle. The bad news is that if a man whose fame was found in the fact that he spoke to God "face to face" could be overcome by anger, so can we. As well, if God did not show special privilege to Moses and give him a second chance, we should expect serious accountability as God's response to our tantrums as well. God places ministers before people to serve them regardless of their stubbornness and meanness. What ministers demonstrate to God's people is received in some ways as a message from God Himself. The minister must take great pains to see to it that they portray in word and deed that our God is patient, full of loving kindness and slow to anger.

Stress and Worry: "Be anxious for nothing…" (Paul from prison; Philippians 4:6). Stress is a major factor for ministers leaving their posts. Little is written about the immense burden that church leaders carry for their congregations. Few things in life are more stressful than the ministry. It is due to the immense burden that ministers must carry along with the eternal weight of what they do. Anxiety is another natural emotion that is felt by everyone at one time or another. Even Jesus felt stress, and to a point that none other has known when praying in Gethsemane. Indeed, Paul's description of the minister in 2 Corinthians 4 reaches out to those sinking in stress and worry. The word *perplexed* is a great description of someone who is suffering from stress and worry.

As Paul revealed more than once, he suffered great amounts of stress. Aside from the painful reality that he was a persecutor of Christ and His church, consider the following incidents that Paul carried with him every day of his life. He was hated, beaten, infirmed with a "thorn in the flesh" that God would not remove, abandoned by Demas, accused by the Jews, undermined by the Judaizers, and encouraged by only a select few. If ministry was a popularity contest, Paul was losing big time! However, he not only dealt with the issues as they arose, but he also continued to thrive in ministry. Think of some of the general truths that we learn from Paul (along with what has been previously discussed in the Miletus speech) that can aid a minister in overcoming worry and stress in the ministry.

1. Let the love of Christ control you (2 Corinthians 5:14).
2. Recognize nothing according to the flesh (2 Corinthians 5:16).

3. Do everything in the Spirit (pray, worship, walk, be filled, etc.).
4. To live is Christ (Philippians 1:21).
5. Consider others as more important than yourself (Philippians 2:3).
6. Show humility, realizing that you've probably done worse to others and have definitely done worse to Christ.
7. Recognize your encouragers and show them appreciation (with Barnabas).
8. Utilize the blessings of fellowship and prayer.
9. Continue to make study and reading an important part of your routine.
10. Keep your perspective by realizing that you are not home yet!
11. Be forgiving, patient, and loving like Christ (Matthew 5:14–15).

Paul, through the Spirit's power and Christ's presence, made a real difference in the life of people from the wealthy and powerful (Caesar's household) to the poor and outcast. He held the Gospel in highest regard and insisted that loving God and loving people were the two reasons that he had been born. From his personal experiences, he also carried an extra motivation with him, the reality of what a zealous person could be without God—a destroyer of the church.

At least a portion of stress and worry that comes with the ministry is self-imposed and was not intended for a human to carry alone. However, there is a very real level of burden, expectation, and accountability that can only be carried by one who finds strength in the greatest power in the universe. His yoke is easy and His burden is light (Matthew 11:30).

Culminating in Depression

Only a specific individual and God can understand the pressures of any given life. Ministry is no exception to this rule. Church work is among the most rewarding and most emotionally and spiritually challenging jobs a person can hold in this life. One recent survey states that over 70% of active ministers struggle with depression.[21] It is an ancient problem that continues to have very little advice regarding a cure.

When you think about spiritual depression, you think of loneliness and isolation. When you think of ministers, you realize that there is little or no chance of them separating themselves from people. These people are often struggling with similar stress, frustration, perceived failure, and depression. The result is a complex situation that makes working through depression an even more complex endeavor for everyone. Ministers can be depressed for various reasons and at various times. How one gets out of such a rut is just as much of a mystery. The reality that so many ministers suffer from this would logically lead one to believe that it is the culmination of the high expectations that people hold in regard to the minister, the endless job that the ministry is, the heavy burden that is carried, and the sense of inadequacy and failure that follows much of ministry.

In the Bible, we see people depressed. It is clear that both Job and the writer of Ecclesiastes were living through a deep depression. Both of these instances come from Old Testament wisdom literature, which emphasizes a deep reflection of life. The rest of the Bible seems to speak very little about depression. Even so, the New Testament believer still struggles with this most painful issue and the only true path out is through the cross.

Is there a light at the end of the tunnel? There is indeed! There are a few things to keep in mind. First, do not go and make things worse by abandoning your ministerial purpose in life. When dealing with depression and frustration, it is not good to make life-changing decisions. Stay the course until your mind clears enough to think soberly. Don't move until you know that God has spoken and that you've accomplished what you've been called to do. If you've not written a farewell speech, begin to make a list of things that you know God has called you to do in your current place of service. This is a great exercise. Trust me, I know.

Second, reach out for help. God has put people in your life as anchors and wise counselors; all you have to do is remember that they are there. You may feel alone, but you are not. Meet on a regular basis with a fellow minister from a different church, your associational missionary (or DOM), a former college or seminary professor, or friend. Make sure that you talk regularly with your spouse and, if you are so blessed, with your parents as well. Prayer—good, honest, and broken prayer is a huge step in the right direction. The key to working through depression is knowing that you are in it and that although you feel like you are alone, there is nothing farther from the truth.

Third, read the Word. During these times, you will see it in a different light. It will have a more profound impact on you. David's imprecatory Psalms make much more sense, Job's happy ending of seeing God becomes more meaningful, you will marvel at how Joseph lasted two years in jail with only the knowledge that God was in control, and you will realize that this portion of your life's ministry may be very difficult to swallow, but it brings you into a more real knowledge of God than you have ever had before.

Fourth, understand that God may not take your "thorn in the flesh" away. Scholars have often mused on what Paul's weakness may have been. God believes that it is much more beneficial to us to not know the specifics! It may have been a physical infirmity, but it doesn't take much to realize that depression can be just as debilitating. You may not have the cloud lift for quite some time. God may remain silent as well. He will, however, be found of you when you seek Him with all of your heart (Jeremiah 29:13–14).

Finally, you must move forward in such times. Continue marching to the last orders you received from Him. One foot in front of the other and one day at a time, march. Let God's promises be enough.

Let His presence be enough. Let your worship of Him continue. You may not be overjoyed in what you are doing, but obedience is better than sacrifice (1 Samuel 15:22). Your following of God's call is essential. It is the only way to climb the vast mountain before you. That was what Ecclesiastes teaches us in the end, life does not just feel futile and meaningless, it actually is! However, an eternal perspective of God's glory (fear Him) and our call (obey Him) is all that will move us forward.

With nearly three out of every four ministers suffering from depression, it is really hard to believe that no one has found a way to wake themselves up from the nightmare. Perhaps it is that the basics work in all situations. If there is sin in our lives, repent of it. If there is anger at God, humble yourself and rethink your flawed theology. If you lack wisdom, ask of God (James 1:5). If you do not know what else to do to the people that have wronged you, make a move that is always legal, demonstrate to them the fruit of the Spirit. Love, joy, peace, patience, kindness, gentleness, and self-control are always the correct response (Galatians 5:22–23).

All of these difficult emotions are a natural solution to life's struggles. However, they are not spiritual ones. Paul instructs that it is up to us to get rid of it. "Let all bitterness and wrath and anger and clamor and slander be put away from you, along with all malice" (Ephesians 4:31). We are not that kind of people, and when people see us live by a different "set of rules," they are pointed toward our Prince of Peace.

Conclusion: The Dreaded Meeting

Remember the meeting that this chapter opened with? The anxiety, the pain, the painful anticipation of a ministry ended? Perhaps some of you have lived through this day in the past or anticipate it in the future. However, the reason for your grief may not be determined yet. Although it could be a discussion of a severance package, an airing of grievances, and a taking of sides, it could also be something better, a heartfelt good-bye. The man we were looking at was not any pastor; in fact he was no pastor at all. He was an apostle. His grief was defined by personal pain that sprouted from love, not anger. His feeling of depression was not based in feeling trapped, but rather that he had to go. Notice the reaction of the Ephesian elders after Paul had delivered his farewell speech.

> When he had said these things, he knelt down and prayed with them all. And they began to weep aloud and embraced Paul, and repeatedly kissed him, grieving especially over the word which he had spoken, that they would not see his face again. And they were accompanying him to the ship. (Acts 20:36–38)

Picture this scene as your own. Pursue it. It can be yours if you will work through the difficult times in your ministry. Trust in God's call, love His people, and allow forgiveness and healing to take place in all situations.

Jesus prayed for His disciples and us. "That they may all be one; even as You, Father, *are* in Me and I in You, that they also may be in Us, so that the world may believe that You sent Me" (John 17:21). The bottom line is that early exits from ministries may be among the main reasons that American churches are not healthy and growing. Few today know that God sent Christ because His disciples are not unified (John 17:20–21). Press forward, push through, and allow God to do His best work!

4

Be a Man of the Word (Acts 20:20–21, 26)

The Bible is God's self-disclosure. Everything we need to know about Him—from His role in our existence to His plan for our lives—He revealed to us through these sixty-six books written by these greatly diverse human authors who were moved by God to write the words that we now know as God-breathed. During his good-bye to the Ephesian elders, Paul stated with great confidence that he made a priority of being a man of the Word in their midst. This was a goal, and he had met it. He knew what we all must accept—if a minister has not trained the people in the Word, we have left them defenseless in our absence.

Although there is no playbook for genuine revival or a perfect church, all true revivals and healthy churches have had the Bible at the forefront. From the Great Commission to the Protestant Reformation and the Great Awakening, those movements, ministers, and congregations that take the Bible seriously are the ones that God has blessed. It is nearly impossible to overplay the role of Scripture in a healthy church and/or ministry. In what the minister teaches and preaches—in what he counsels and prescribes, the Scriptures are foundational to eternal success. For the minister, the Bible has to be fundamental to methodology, strategy, and practice of ministry. Nowhere is this seen more clearly than from the pulpit and the podium. The preaching and teaching ministries of the healthy church are prominent. God blesses the church that honors His timeless truths. A look at these guiding principles will guide in our effort to be "a man of the Word."

The Bible is a Miracle

The Bible—although our greatest path to truth—remains an enigma in many ways. Clearly, it has a life all its own. One of the greatest quotes about the Bible comes from Bernard Ramm, it makes this point abundantly clear.

> A thousand times over, the death knell of the Bible has been sounded, the funeral procession formed, the inscription cut on the tombstone, and committal read. But somehow the corpse never stays put. No other book has been so chopped, knived, sifted, scrutinized, and vilified. What book on philosophy or religion or psychology or *belles lettres* of classical or modern times has been subject to such a mass attack as the Bible? with such venom and skepticism? with such thoroughness and erudition? upon every chapter, line, and tenet? The Bible is still loved by millions, read by millions, and studied by millions.[22]

It is quite amazing that generations of skeptics, critics, and those who devote their lives toward the destruction of the Bible's credibility have still yet to gain mainstream momentum. The biblical critic is no match for the written Word.

The Bible is completely unique, divine, and overpowering. It is among the greatest miracles of Christianity. God continues to speak to us through it on a daily basis. It is the Word that brought us to our calling as ministers, and it is the Word that must see us through it. When the time comes, it is the Word that must reign authoritative in our methods, mission, and exits.

The Bible was Written to be Proclaimed

Undoubtedly, Christianity is better off with preaching, and the ministry of proclamation will continue to play a central role in the future of the Christian church until the return of Christ. It remains "the greatest act in connection with the church and her function."[23] The reasons for such assertions are many. However, even with a great understanding of the importance of preaching, the preacher often forgets one of the most important details—the preacher must preach to himself first.

Far too many ministers do not place themselves as a part of the congregation when the sermon is being prepared. The result is a sermon from the preacher to the congregation and not a message from God to the church. There is an obvious difference between the two. Preachers who preach to themselves are more humble, their sermons more reflective, and their application more profound.

Nothing is more insightful nor draws a minister closer to the congregation than sharing your spiritual journey with them. Too much detail can be detrimental, but giving the congregation a good feel for where you are, where you have been, and where you are going, lets them know that you trust them as family and that allows them to reciprocate. This method assists the process of love between the minister and congregation and thus allows for more effective worship, evangelism, and ministry.

There has always been a great chasm between preachers who care about both the sermon and the congregation and those who care mainly about one or the other. The great preachers of church history held both in high esteem.

> Not a one of them (influential preachers) was lost in abstract theology, aimless piety, or ranting exhortation. There is no artificial division in their preaching between 'ethics' and 'evangelism.' The essential fact is–they cared. They cared about people, their pain and grief–whether spiritual, physical, moral, or social–and they addressed themselves to that; sometimes through sermons that sought to teach the way

of God through doctrine, sometimes through sermons that sought to tell men about a better life through evangelistic preaching, and sometimes through sermons that brought the judgment of God upon the institutions of men by ethical preaching.[24]

Preachers have defined and will continue to define the direction of the church first by their character but also through their methodologies and convictions concerning both the Bible and their congregation.

The Holy Spirit is the Expert on Scripture

The Holy Spirit wrote Scripture. If we are to truly understand the truth of the Bible, we need to consult the author. He knows its intention and its application. Unless the Spirit anoints both the study and proclaiming of the Scriptures, only minimal gain will result.

The Spirit's anointing is usually the missing ingredient when a pulpit ministry is having difficulty. Even so, very little discussion has taken place regarding the Holy Spirit's anointing within a sermon. What has taken place has found little agreement. It is clear that the anointing is beyond the normal move of the Spirit in Bible study, it is an empowering and revealing move that allows insights to be gained that were not of the preacher's wisdom. When the Spirit moves, the preacher and many congregants know it. Consider the following descriptions of this supernatural event.

> He can make you feel your subject till it thrills you, and you become depressed by it so as to be crushed to the earth, or elevated by it so as to be borne upon its eagle wings; making you feel, besides your subject, your object, till you yearn for the conversion of men, and for the uplifting of Christians to something nobler than they have known as yet…all of this will be going on during the discourse.[25]

Another similar definition is given by D. Martyn Lloyd-Jones.

> What is this (the unction)? It is the Holy Spirit falling upon the preacher in a special manner. It is an access of power. It is a God giving power, and enabling, through the Spirit, to the preacher in order that he may do this work in a manner that lifts it up beyond the efforts and endeavors of man to a position in which the preacher is being used by the Spirit and becomes the channel through whom the Spirit works. This is seen very plainly and clearly in the Scriptures.[26]

Lloyd-Jones notes that even for the disciples, just being around Jesus and hearing all that He said was not enough to constitute the anointing. It is a special move of the Spirit beyond the norm of His consistent work through the illumining of the Word that happens for a special, heavenly purpose.

With this in mind, one fellow preacher exhorts the minister to "enter a contract with the Holy Spirit" that submits our will to His and allows our bodies to be used by Him.[27] It is clear that the Spirit's work throughout the process of biblical proclamation is imperative. It is also equally clear that a consensus on how this is done is not currently within reach. Even so, the Spirit should not only be welcomed into this process but also implored to make it His own.

Only Certain People are Willing to Listen to Its Truth

Another key rule for preaching is that the minister must address who is there. Although our sermons should have an evangelistic flavor and focus to them, we must remember to address the people who are actually sitting in the pews. Give them a more profound understanding of the Word, of God's character, of the life of a "spiritual priest." Keep in mind that these are the people that God's

Spirit has already been working on. They are there and are most likely at least open to knowing God through His self-revelation.

We must also keep in mind that most unchurched people do not care too much for the Bible and most likely never will unless we reach them and God reveals Himself through this process. Statistics are abundantly clear that evangelistic preaching is less effective than personal evangelism is. Fewer people in today's world walk the aisle under conviction from a passion-filled sermon. More are coming to the Lord because God worked through other ways. On the other hand, statistics do support that a great amount of discipleship comes through preaching. Note this C.S. Lewis quote:

> In most parts of the Bible, everything is implicitly or explicitly introduced with 'Thus saith the Lord'. It is… not merely a sacred book but a book so remorselessly and continuously sacred that it does not invite—it excludes or repels—the merely aesthetic approach. You can read it as literature only by a tour de force… It demands incessantly to be taken on its own terms: it will not continue to give literary delight very long, except to those who go to it for something quite different. I predict that it will in the future be read, as it always has been read, almost exclusively by Christians.[28]

Far too many pastors use other successful ministers for a model when their context is nothing like that of the successful pastors. Going with the earlier logic that a sermon is a discussion between God and the congregation (including the pastor), it would make sense that, unless one has a large number of lost people each week, most sermons would address the Christians who are there. No doubt, evangelistic preaching has a legitimate place, but unless it's producing great numbers of converts each month, the minister may need to consider what God wants to say to the people that showed up ready to listen.

Orthodoxy is Edgy

We do live in curious times indeed! In recent years, we have seen churches try most everything to get folks to show up. We have offered them gifts, preached what they wanted to hear, marketed ourselves to death, and changed basically everything in the church from furniture to the place in the service where we take up the offering. Although some things have worked, many others have not. While we stand with success stories on one side trumpeting the new direction, we have critics on the other decrying the effect such methodologies have on the effectiveness of the Gospel. Most pastors and scholars know that many things can change in a church that will allow God to move freely outside of the restrictions of human tradition. We also know that things can go overboard, and with sinful humans, they often do.

If the Bible is God's Word, then it must be the central resource for church methodology. We must remember that the Bible is the most "edgy" book, the most relevant book, and the most valuable book ever written about the most "edgy," relevant, and valuable person, message, and hope ever known. The Bible doesn't need help becoming relevant, it already is! Now, that's not to say that all sermons are! Entire books have been written about this subject, but it should suffice to say that if the Bible is loved by the minister, consumed by the minister, effective for change in the life of the minister, that the sermon will be a profound, insightful, Spirit-empowered delight to most all of those in the congregation.

If ministers want to be nontraditional, they must not attempt to follow cultural trends, but rather Jesus himself. Some ministers insist on drinking a casual brew, others insist on talking incessantly about sex from the pulpit while still others attempt to say things to knock their congregations back. However, Jesus's controversy was based in His claims, not in craving attention or a need for controversy. It is not about what we can do, but what the minister ought to do.[29]

Clearly, there is a difference between being disliked for orthodoxy's sake and being unwelcomed because you are a person that has controversy following you wherever you go. Think for a moment what were the "controversies" that made Jesus "edgy"? It was not the fact that He drank wine. Nor was it that He talked about sex. Nor was it that He refused to be involved with the established church/religion. I would say that Jesus was most controversial for His claims to Deity. That is what got Him killed! He claimed the authority that He rightfully had. This was the larger issues behind the smaller criticisms. While we often seem to focus on the "he eats with sinners" accusation, we forget that it was the decentralizing of spiritual power that brought Him the most pain. For Him it was not political, it was personal. Jesus healed, cared, prayed, proclaimed, stood up for the helpless, reached out to those of another race, culture, social strata, etc. It was His teachings on redemption, forgiveness, the pride of man, the will of God, and the call to love each other that brought Him the fame that got Him crucified.

If a minister was to love the unloved like Jesus did, not by simply having a beer with them, but by going to battle with Satan over their soul, wouldn't that cause a stir? If a pastor refused to show preference to the wealthy families with the cute kids and the nice houses, wouldn't that cause a bit of uneasiness? Perhaps, if a minister forgave those who are trying to run him off, went to them in private with a broken heart and sought reconciliation, wouldn't that shake the very foundation of authority in the church? Maybe it works, maybe it doesn't. Some would say that Christ failed, but we know differently. Only time will tell in our ministries.

People are drawn by circuses, events, epics, smackdowns, and the like. However, there is a universe of difference between drawing a crowd and building a church. Let the Spirit draw your people with the "edge" of orthodoxy, the insanity of unconditional forgiveness, and the scandalous controversy of unrequited love found in the Gospel (1 Corinthians 1:23).

The Path to Orthodoxy

Of all of the things that many preachers might believe they are, including prophet, lecturer, counselor, friend, and theologian, nothing captures the true biblical calling of the preacher more than the title steward. The preacher is a steward of God's mysteries and revelation that is found in the Scriptures.[30] Being the sole occupier of the congregation's pulpit, the methodology of the preacher in preparation and delivery is crucial to the growth and vitality of the church. Sermons must be, above all else, a statement of objective, authoritative, and eternal truth. Therefore, it is the consensus of many of the great pulpiteers that preaching should be expository.[31] Lloyd-Jones summarizes this sentiment, "I would emphasize again that while doing all this you must *always* be expository. *Always* expository…the matter should always be derived from Scriptures, it should *always* be expository."[32] Clearly, it is the most appropriate method for one who wishes to give the clearest thrust, points, and context of the text itself.

The problem does remain, however, even among proponents of expository preaching, that many who think that they are expository preachers are clearly not. Many assume that biblical preaching and/or textual preaching is the same as expository preaching. For them, being nontopical is equivalent to being expository. Faris Whitesell makes a clear distinction between expository and all other kinds of sermons.

> In the expository approach, we study not only the roots, trunk and branches of our tree (as does the textual method), we also consider its leaves, soil, climate, inner ring system, distinctive features, life history, and relation to other trees and vegetation around it, the uses to which we can put this tree, and how to reproduce this tree and others like it not only here, but in other parts of the world. In other words, we seek a comprehensive, detailed and thorough knowledge of our tree. From the mass of information which we compile, we arrange our expository talk about our tree. We find a subject,

a theme, a thesis, a logical outline, and a sound development. We may not use all of the material we have gathered, but we use most of it. This is the expository method.[33]

If a comprehensive understanding of the text is desired, this is the method that most naturally will provide such an outcome.

Plainly, the closer a sermon is tied to the biblical text, the more effective and eternal it will be. "When we say what God says, we have authority."[34] There are many reasons for believing that expository preaching best accomplishes this. First, expository preaching is wed to the text. Second, it limits the scope of the subject matter. Third, expositional preaching is easier for the hearer to follow. Fourth, it limits the preacher's personal input and opinion. Finally, it offers the preacher the greatest effectiveness for the ministry. It is a true hallmark of a growing and healthy church.[35] Indeed, expository preaching solidifies the maturation and expansion of the congregation. It is the best way for us to be "stewards of the mysteries of God."

Cherish Your Time in the Pulpit

Nothing can stop a preacher from loving the pulpit unless the minister lets it. It is natural for a pastor to love to preach. While proclaiming the Word is not always easy, it is most likely not as difficult in your situation as it is for other pastors in hostile countries on any given Sunday. Church history is full of Godly men who refused to stop preaching: Peter, Stephen, Paul, Hugh Latimer, Thomas Cranmer, Dietrich Bonhoeffer, and thousands of others (even up to this day) and have paid the ultimate price. The pulpit cannot be minimized or neglected because of ministerial strife. It serves as aid and comfort to the church and a genuine threat to the enemy.

Although it cost him dearly, Paul tells the Ephesian elders that he "did not shrink back from declaring anything…that was profitable." While many reduce this act to preaching, the apostle noted that this particular ministry was both public and intimate. It was through the ministry of the Word that he grew quite close to the Ephesians Christians. Once you establish (or reestablish) your preaching ministry, the door is opened wide for you to share your passion for God's Word through teaching and counseling. The Bible is desperately needed today in a pluralistic society where lines are drawn between reason and faith. God warned Israel through Hosea, "my people are destroyed for lack of knowledge…" Do not let ignorance be the destructive force that takes down the people that God has placed under your supervision. Expository preaching returns the topic of discussion back to the Bible.

When the pastor is a man of the Word, people will begin to pick up their own habits from his example and follow down his path. Without a clear conviction and passion regarding the proclamation of the authoritative biblical witness, the church will be rendered defenseless against the enemy's attacks. However, with the establishment of truth, the church will not only be preserved but will also thrive in the generations before Christ's return.

It is never too late in your ministry to rekindle your flame with God. You can worship Him with more meaning in your pain, and you can fall in love with His Word and its proclamation all over again! The pulpit is such a mysterious and beautiful time where God and the minister meet with the congregation. The Spirit only gets this opportunity to pour Himself in to a man so many times in a human lifespan. Nothing is more satisfying than pouring yourself into a sermon than feeling the exhaustion of a week's worth of hard labor when the sermon is done. Few greater joys exist than seeing the eyes of congregants come to life at the Word's truth. Some are brought to tears, others to unspeakable joy, but God is talking to His kids—there is nothing more beautiful than that. I implore you, don't waste a Sunday.

5

Be Humble and Selfless (Acts 20:22–24)

There are many things that God desires from His people and most of these are offerings that we don't want to bring. At times it is because we don't make a priority of giving God what we have, at other times it is because we don't actually have them to give. It stands to reason that you cannot give away something you don't possess. This is the issue at hand with regard to selflessness and humility. However, these attributes can be a "game changer" in the Christian life and ministry if we have them.

Although humility has never been in fashion, it is nearly extinct in postmodern America. The prospects of people—let alone a community—embracing the call toward humility is made even less likely in a society where self-promotion is seemingly the only way to get ahead, where one has little interest in kneeling before anything, and denying oneself is only for delayed gratification. True, biblical Christianity is a hard sell in any individualistic society. That is why Christianity remains the fastest growing world religion, everywhere but in America and a few other self-focused societies.[36] Communism, despotism, and persecution cannot hinder the Gospel, but selfish societies always have. Jesus set down the first law of discipleship in very clear terms, "If anyone desires to be my disciple, he must first deny himself..." Ministers are expected to set the example in humility and self-denial. Their inability to do so is often one of many reasons that the burden of ministry becomes too difficult to bear.

It is an undeniable reality that humility is often lacking in born leaders, even Christian ones. It is also not breaking news that humility is mandatory. Rather than making an argument for something that we all agree is imperative, let a review suffice to remind us of this most serious calling. A look at those in Scripture who were prideful, as well as those who were humble, will give clear direction to our path's end.

Arrogant Leaders in Scripture

Unfortunately, one does not have to be a Bible scholar to readily identify those leaders in Scripture who thought more highly of themselves than they should have. Begin with Adam and Eve's thirst for forbidden knowledge and their son Cain refusing to be his "brother's keeper" and go from there. Stories of arrogance litter the pages of Scripture.

Have you ever considered what type of leaders allowed society to sink to the depths before the flood was required? Think about the leadership who encouraged the people that staying together and building a tower as an affront to God was a good idea? Pharaoh's arrogance cost him his nation, his people, and his own son. Solomon's pride led his heart away from the God he *knew* to be real. Herod was a horrible king who made a joke of Christ's presence and the plight of his own people. The Beast in Revelation will exercise the ultimate act of pride and demand worship from his people as did Antiochus Epiphanes. From beginning to end, pride is employed by many leaders, and it always ends in serious damage to both the leader and those for whom they are responsible.

Throughout history, many prideful kings lost their throne, authority, legacy, family, and their very lives because of their inability to humble themselves, even the slightest bit, before an all-powerful God. Pride has become the standard, and we in America have crowned it a new "virtue." Because kings and kingdoms seem so far removed from the ministry, we often disassociate ourselves from the problem of pride.

It is not the pride of Pharaoh or Herod that destroys preachers. It is rather a much more silent and simple pride that takes us down. It is a pride that results in self-pity and bitterness instead of delusions of grandeur. When unchecked, these self-centered and prideful convictions result in plots of vengeance at worse or rejoicing in other's failures at best. This is the "antihumility" that destroys ministry. We see this clearly through specific examples in biblical history.

Ahithophel is an interesting guy. He hated King David, I mean really hated King David. He wanted him either humiliated or dead, but preferred both. Second Samuel 17:23 tells of this man's less than glorious end. "Now when Ahithophel saw that his counsel was not followed, he saddled his donkey and arose and went to his home, to his city, and set his house in order, and strangled himself; thus he died and was buried in the grave of his father." What is most disturbing about this man is that he was highly respected for his wisdom. In fact, talking to Ahithophel was like talking to God Himself (2 Samuel 16:23). He was an advisor to David, it was Israel's "Camelot"—what more could he ever want!

We see, as the story progresses, Ahithophel chooses to support David's rebellious son, Absalom, in his attempt to usurp his father's throne. When David learned of this, he prayed that God would make Ahithophel's advice seem foolish to Absalom, fearing that this wise counselor would devise a devastating plan to bring David's kingdom crashing down. Not surprisingly, Absalom's new adviser gave him words that could have given him the kingdom! He instructed him to go into his father's concubines and lay with them (which he did) and then send an army of twelve thousand to take David down. Ahithophel even volunteered to take this regiment himself, offering both legitimacy to the assassins and a front-row seat for Ahithophel to witness the demise of the king. It was a brilliant strategy![37] As Samuel informs the reader, this advice was rejected for a much-less sound approach of Absalom leading all of the men he could find across many forests to crush David. This was given by a loyalist of the king and was accepted for its grandeur. It was when his counsel was rejected that Ahithophel went home and ended his life. In the end, David continued to reign and Absalom died in humility.

What was the deal with Ahithophel? Why was he so angry at David? This is one of those situations where it may be difficult to tell, but there is a possibility that it had something to do with his granddaughter. Now, all "papas" think their grandbabies are cute. However, God's Word itself tells us that Ahithophel's granddaughter was indeed quite stunning.

> Now when evening came David arose from his bed and walked around on the roof of the king's house, and from the roof he saw a woman bathing; and the woman was *very beautiful* in appearance. So David sent and inquired about the woman. And one said, 'Is this not Bathsheba, the daughter of Eliam, the wife of Uriah the Hittite?' (2 Samuel 11:2–3)

It is interesting that it was David's disregard for his family, his murdering of Uriah, and his unethical treatment of the power that God had given him that obsessed one of his closest confidants to destroy him through a patient, purposeful, and devious plot. Here we note that Bathsheba's father was Eliam, and Eliam's father was named Ahithophel (2 Samuel 23:34). This would indeed explain Ahithophel's bitter anger toward the king and his insistence on his humiliation and death. Ahithophel's silent pride, his underhanded vendetta, and his abuse of wisdom made him an enemy of God. If David did not execute him, God would take care of the traitor himself.

Whatever it may have been, the bitterness that led to vengeance is still the reality that had destroyed one of the greatest advisors of the Davidic kingdom. Honestly, he was already under judgment before David's life was spared, he just did not care. Second, everyone in the kingdom had a right to be angry with David. His betrayal of Uriah was inexcusable. The problem arises when one believes that God cannot discipline His own either through divine intervention or through the procedures He's set in place. God already had taken care of the problem. Finally, it was not David, but pride that destroyed and ultimately killed Ahithophel as was the case with Haman in Esther's day. The path of forgiveness, truth, and reconciliation might have afforded both Ahithophel and Absalom a longer, more peaceful life.

We can look at many more people whose pride destroyed their ministries. Jonah was indeed one of those. Others include the Levite priest of Judges who allowed his concubine to be savaged and murdered (Judges 19), Hananiah who went against the truth of God's prophecy given through Jeremiah (Jeremiah 28), as well as Demas, Paul's companion, whose love of the things of this world ripped him away from the faith (2 Timothy 4:10). Indeed, there is no shortage of examples that lost confidence, position, health, and even life because of their own stubborn and prideful hearts.

The Call to Humility

It is important to note that when the Bible commands something repeatedly, it reveals two truths. First, we have to be told to do it because it is contrary to our nature, and second, God has to keep reminding us because we are prone to forget or disregard the expectation. The expectation of humility is clear. Without it, God cannot bless people. In fact, He is forced to reject them, to discipline them, and to allow them to fall.

Consider some of these verses that clearly demonstrate the call toward a humble life and the rebuke of a prideful person.

- You rebuke the arrogant, who are cursed and who stray from your commands (Psalms 119:21).
- Though the lord is on high, he looks upon the lowly, but the proud he knows from afar (Psalms 138:6).

- The lord sustains the humble but casts the wicked to the ground (Psalms 147:6).
- He mocks proud mockers but gives grace to the humble (Proverbs 3:34).
- When pride comes, then comes disgrace, but with humility comes wisdom (Proverbs 11:2).
- Pride goes before destruction, a haughty spirit before a fall. Better to be lowly in spirit and among the oppressed than to share plunder with the proud (Proverbs 16:18–19).
- He guides the humble in what is right and teaches them his way (Proverbs 25:9).
- Has not my hand made all these things, and so they came into being?" declares the lord. "This is the one I esteem: he who is humble and contrite in spirit, and trembles at my word" (Isaiah 66:2).
- He has showed you, O man, what is good. And what does the lord require of you? To act justly and to love mercy and to walk humbly with your God (Micah 6:8).
- For whoever exalts himself will be humbled, and whoever humbles himself will be exalted (Matthew 23:12).
- Sitting down, Jesus called the Twelve and said, "If anyone wants to be first, he must be the very last, and the servant of all" (Mark 9:35).
- How can you believe if you accept praise from one another, yet make no effort to obtain the praise that comes from the only God (John 5:44).
- For by the grace given me I say to every one of you: Do not think of yourself more highly than you ought, but rather think of yourself with sober judgment, in accordance with the measure of faith God has given you (Romans 12:3).
- Love is…not proud (1 Corinthians 13:4).

- If I must boast, I will boast of the things that show my weakness (2 Corinthians 11:30).
- Therefore, as God's chosen people, holy and dearly loved, clothe yourselves with compassion, kindness, humility, gentleness and patience (Colossians 3:12).

It does not take a serious study of Scripture to realize that refusing to be humble is refusing God's plan for humanity and is indeed rejecting His own character. When He sent Christ to give us a revelation of Himself, he could not have painted humility more perfectly. Jesus was all-powerful, all-knowing, all-sufficient, and yet a servant. One can see in these verses that the choice of pride over humility is outright rebellion. There are no exceptions to this rule. If a minister does not serve in humility, he cannot serve God.

The Selfless Life

When all is said and done, the bottom line is that Christ was clearly the greatest, wisest, and most effective minister in history. He was also the most humble, and it clearly cost Him everything. When given the opportunity to demonstrate God's method of ministry, Jesus served in humility in every aspect of His calling. Even when he rebuked, He did it in humility. No serious critic accused Him of a power grab or of politics. Instead, He is known as the miracle worker, the lover of sinners, the washer of feet, and the giver of hope. Recall these great words of truth proclaimed in this first-century hymn, used by Paul to encourage an attitude of service and humility.

> Therefore if there is any encouragement in Christ, if there is any consolation of love, if there is any fellowship of the Spirit, if any affection and compassion, make my joy complete by being of the same mind, maintaining the same love, united in spirit, intent on one purpose. Do nothing from selfishness or empty conceit, but with humility of mind regard one

another as more important than yourselves; do not merely look out for your own personal interests, but also for the interests of others. Have this attitude in yourselves which was also in Christ Jesus, who, although He existed in the form of God, did not regard equality with God a thing to be grasped, but emptied Himself, taking the form of a bond-servant, and being made in the likeness of men. Being found in appearance as a man, He humbled Himself by becoming obedient to the point of death, even death on a cross. For this reason also, God highly exalted Him, and bestowed on Him the name which is above every name, so that at the name of Jesus every knee will bow, of those who are in heaven and on earth and under the earth, and that every tongue will confess that Jesus Christ is Lord, to the glory of God the Father. (Philippians 2:1–11)

No greater example of humility exists than our Savior. As well, no greater motivation should be needed. Paul adopted Christ as his model for ministry, "But I do not consider my life of any account as dear to myself, so that I may finish my course and the ministry which I received from the Lord Jesus, to testify solemnly of the gospel of the grace of God." Paul got it! Even though Paul—like many pastors today—was a roaring lion in personality, he was able to serve with humility in the name of Christ. A quick look at how he made this transition will enable us to make similar transitions. Note the following keys to Paul's humility:

1. *Contentment in all situations of life* including poor health, poverty, ostracizing, and abandonment. Keep in mind Paul's acceptance of God's refusal to remove his thorn in flesh. He responded with, "I will glory in my weakness so that Christ may be strong through me." (2 Corinthians 12:7–10). As well, he encouraged Timothy to recognize that godliness with contentment was the point where an individual began to make gains in life (2 Timothy 6:6).

2. *Forgiveness of those who've wronged him* and forgetting past difficulties. While being a lion, Paul worked on moving forward. In the third chapter of Philippians, he speaks of his difficulties being minimized in his pursuit of Christ. He summarizes by stating, "I forget what is behind and press toward the mark" (Philippians 3:14).

3. *Christ is the meaning of life.* This reality motivated Paul toward Holiness. He believed that God was in Christ and Christ was in us. Because of this, Christ was our life (Colossians 3:4). Paul had died when Christ died, he lived only because Jesus was alive. He was ready to die but willing to stay. He wanted only the words of affirmation from Christ and no one else. He was the very definition of a bond slave, he lived to please his master.

4. *Love overpowered hate and conquered all* (wrath, disunity, a multitude of sins). Love has unfortunately been "punted" to the liberals in recent decades. Conservatives are afraid to even speak of it for fear of sounding shallow or overemotional. However, God is love (1 John 4:8) and love never fails (1 Corinthians 13:8). As well, love is the key to many things including forgiveness, reconciliation, serving, and worship. Sin kills, but love covers a multitude of sins (1 Peter 4:8). It was the substance of the two greatest commandments. It is the first fruit of the Holy Spirit and must be first priority in the lives of all believers, especially ministers.

5. *Prayer is key.* Although we learned the model of prayer from the Lord's Prayer, we see Jesus's ultimate prayer of intercession in John 17 and prayer of submission in Gethsemane. To build on this, Paul teaches us that prayer is an essential tool for the ministry. He prayed for his churches that they would grow in Christ and grow in love toward one another. He made God's call central to intercession. Note his prayers at the beginning of Philippians and Ephesians particularly.

6. *A clear understanding of his calling.* Paul stated clearly that Christian ministers are "ministers of reconciliation" and ambassadors for Christ (2 Corinthians 5:19–20). His call was one of suffering, mixed with missions, preaching, and debating for the truth. He was always ready, focused, and, therefore, effective. His goal was God's goal, to bring a wandering people back to God. He lived by the two great commandments and the Great Commission.

7. *The Word was his lifeline.* Paul realized that God's Word was alive. He was a scholar of the law and was very familiar with the Gospel of Christ. His life was centered around what God had revealed. As a result of this, he encouraged Timothy, among all things, to be a minister of the Word of God.

Although not complete, this list of Pauline's attitudes toward ministry must be adopted as our own. It is this that keeps us focused on the eternal and will keep us humble and selfless in the meantime. The more that our emphasis is on the big picture, the smaller our focus will be on the insignificant and noneternal. Perhaps, with God's grace, we ministers can bring humility back into fashion!

6

Leave Things Better than You Found Them (Acts 20:28–32)

As a seminary student, I remember anxiously waiting for my first "real" church. I envisioned great things. Numbers were at the top of my list, of course. These included "noble numbers" like baptisms, new members, and multimillion-dollar budgets. Along with this was a foolproof strategy that would both disciple and equip the members to do my job for me. I was also planning on early retirement. Well, actual experiences rarely meet expectations. However, sound words of wisdom broke through these unrealistic goals with one exhortation from a professor. "Just don't mess things up!" he said. "Be sure to leave things better than you found them." Although this may seem the words of a negative-minded critic of church ministry, the reality that many churches are wounded and that there will undoubtedly be a time when you will have to exit make these words very sound advice. They should hit us hard, and we should take them to heart.

What the pastor must do to make the church stronger is prepare them for the future, focus down the road, and help them to be strong in their calling and gifts and not ours. Like Paul, we should take an approach to ministry that keeps in mind our predecessor and the one who comes after us. Paul recognized the efforts of Apollos, Dorcas and others and realized that an unknown minister would follow him wherever he served. Notice the care he gave to Timothy in Ephesus. A team approach that reaches beyond our tenure (in both directions) is the most effective way to "not mess things up"! Through this effort we can give them a community—focus, better vision, and equipping them to do the work that God has laid before them.

A Community Focus

It is an unfortunate reality that many churches do not know what they are called to do. They go to church, some tithe, some teach, most everyone sings and tries to stay awake, but regarding a clear understanding of the divine expectation on their church, they just don't get it. Community has lost out to the individual, so no one even asks the questions of corporate purpose anymore. There are two key things that must be done to give the church a better focus. First, emphasize individual calling only in light of the church's overall calling. Second, emphasize loyalty and commitment by demonstrating the special position that the church holds within the heart of our Heavenly Father.

We are not lacking the tools to help an individual discover their calling. We have spiritual gift inventories, books, training sessions, premade sermons, and Sunday School lessons galore. However, due to the overemphasis on the individual, the community gets left behind. Even if a parishioner knows what they are called to do, they have no idea how it fits into the call of the church. We have divided everything by age and interest and this has seriously disrupted our focus on multiple levels.

In a survey taken a couple of years back, people were actually found to be more loyal to their brand of toothpaste and toilet paper than they are to their denominational identity.[38] This is both shocking and sad but not necessarily surprising. The disappearance of community, orthodoxy, and loyalty has caused most denominations to crumble. As things trickle down, churches have lost their footing because the individual parishioners do not give her their loyalty. However, in our emphasis to give the individual acknowledgement, we have inadvertently harmed the body. The *church* is Jesus's wife, not you or me, but *we*. We tend to sacrifice this fact at the altar of individuality. Few churches show harmony in purpose and because of that, they show no unified vision either.

In an individualistic society, we see all things played to the advantage of self. Church is clearly no exception to this rule. While many have attempted to create community in the local church, regional church, and universal church, they have not successfully rid the community of individualism. What this has led to is a false community that looks to sentimentally unify but will not make a serious attempt at unification because a true unity demands the death of self. We are left then with only words and no real hopes of community.

A Better Vision

Vision is a funny thing. Everyone has it, they may not be entirely aware of what it is, but they possess it nonetheless. For most, it is their pursuit of happiness or their children's welfare. For others, it is much less noble or meaningful, but it's there nonetheless. Simply put, it's what they hope to accomplish. Because discernment of calling is at an all-time low, so is our vision. In recent years, church health consultants have encouraged mission and vision statements and many churches have engaged in the process. This trend seems to have helped many ministers as well as the small percentage of lay leaders. Unfortunately, it has stopped there. The real challenge has been found in the transfer of the vision to the laity of the church. There are a few "rules of engagement" that can strengthen the church's understanding of purpose and vision.

1. When you give individual gift inventories, compile them as a group and discuss the makeup of the overall body. What

are your strengths as a church and what are your weaknesses? Take the focus away from the individual.

2. Let the congregation develop its own purpose and vision statements. As an overseer and/or minister, guide them through the process but let them own it. These things must be more than what you learned in seminary or Bible college.
3. Help them to have an objective view of their ministerial history. What has God used in the past? What have they tried (or are continuing) that just is not working?
4. Have more activities that are church-wide during Sunday School, morning worship, etc. Let them see each other from the nursery to the senior adult groups. Have a youth minister that understands he/she must foster the community with the teens.
5. Preach on unity, pray for unity, and work toward unity. It does not happen but through Christ, and we move toward Christ when we move toward His purpose and calling on the church. A sermon series on what the church is supposed to do would be quite helpful. I would suggest a series on the Summary Statements in Acts (6:7, 9:31, 12:24, 16:5, 19:20, 28:30–31). These summaries of the early church are key to understanding what a Spirit-filled church looks like.

It is clear that the answers of what makes a better church are subjective because a church is an organism and has its own individual traits from body to body. Beginning with the biblical call and then moving toward their "personality" is essential. Otherwise, there is danger of a church being driven by what it *feels* called to do and not what it *is* called to do.

Better Equipped

When the time for parting comes, the church and minister should be better equipped for Kingdom work than they were when they first began their ministry together. The fellowship should be sweeter, a passion for the lost should be more evident, worship should be more intimate, and everyone should be more knowledgeable of the Word and more mature in the faith. God's intention for a pastoral/congregational relationship is His glory. A clear understanding of the direction that the Spirit hopes to lead the church is essential. Trying and enduring is not enough, accomplishing God's will as revealed in Scripture is.

Once a purpose and vision are clear, the job becomes more specific on how these two essentials are accomplished. This will be a work in progress, but it is at this point that church becomes fun! People are loving Jesus by trying anything they can to honor him. They are seeking actively to deny themselves for the call to follow Christ. It is at this point that ministers get their second or third winds and congregations find themselves. When the minister leaves, what is left is fond memories rather than bitterness and regrets. More importantly, the church is ready for whatever faces them because they do not need to wait for the next leader to tell them what to do, they will already be busy in the work of their calling when he arrives.

Some Thoughts on Church Health

Discussions in the last few years have moved from church growth to church health. I think this was a needed shift in thinking. Both discussions were needed, but we have become denominations that only recognize numbers and qualify them as success. Although megachurches play an important role in American Evangelicalism, we must remember that a church's health is not defined by the measurements we often choose to use. Clearly, Jesus looked much deeper than we often do, and so we must commit to the same practice. We have got to realize that our overall picture in America is mainly one of small, often family-driven churches in rural communities. Consider the following realities.

- The average church size is under one hundred people.
- Megachurches only make up a very small percentage of churches in America.
- Denominational participation and giving is largely from smaller churches.
- Extremely small churches (usually house churches) are the model addressed specifically in the Bible and where the concepts are more directly applied.

As well, we must also keep in mind some of the common denominators of church health that are so consistent they blur denominational, style, and demographic lines.

1. The Word of God is central to a growing, healthy church. This is due to the reality that there is a high view of Scripture from the pulpit to the pew.
2. Pastors are effective in pastoral care, and they have a genuine concern and love for their congregation. In return, healthy churches appreciate their pastor's efforts and forgive his missteps.
3. The church is committed to an outward-focused strategy and is less concerned with issues such as worship styles, budget meetings, and small personality conflicts. They are confident in who they are and do not desire to become like another body.
4. Theology is important and this affects their methodology. This theology stems from the first point. Theology is only effective if it is biblical and taken from a high view of Scripture.
5. The church has a plan several years into the future.
6. The congregation has a keen awareness of the Holy Spirit's presence and guidance.

7. There is an excitement about the children and youth and a genuine respect and appreciation for the senior adults.
8. The church is focused on expansion into new church plants and missions, some regional and some international.
9. A loving unity among membership. Jesus said this is how the world would know we are His.

It is imperative to realize that none of these traits are "size specific." Any church of any size from "two or more" can do any of these things!

No one can make a church healthy. It is the job of the Holy Spirit alone. However, there are techniques, priorities, and methods that He blesses and others we cannot be so sure about. A move back toward Scripture is the only path toward church health, not just in church government but also in personal behavior, temperament, and relational strength. When God moves, things improve. If the church is to be better than we found it, it will only arrive there if the entire church is totally interested in becoming more effective through a maturing, spiritual transformation.

When discouraged, keep this one fact in mind. God is the one who planted this church, who birthed it, called it, named it, and married it. He is more passionate than we could ever be about her health, and he is more protective of her than we could ever be. God desires to move the church toward health. He is also more effective in persuading than pastors can be. Perhaps the path toward health is a move away from a focus on methodology and procedure and a shift toward worship. God's people know when He's there. He has promised us that He is there when we gather and is more than willing to intensify His presence if we prepare our hearts, families, and churches to receive Him.

7

Be a Colaborer (Acts 20:33–35)

We live in a culture obsessed with image and legacy. Unfortunately, all we do in most cases is talk about these ideals and do not actually work on them in any eternally significant way. Because of this reality, these terms lack both definition and substance. As a result, we throw these terms around and yet they seem to have no real impact in what we do and who we are as a church. Instead, image has become self-esteem and legacy has become nothing more than self-perception. Things are not much better in the church. No one mastered both image and legacy better than Paul, and he gives ministers a clear path to a proper perception of and legacy building for a minister and his ministry. The journey can be strenuous, but the concept is actually quite simple, Paul worked hard, kept his word, and considered others as more important than himself.

Before Paul left the Ephesians, he wanted to remind them of a small part of the legacy that he had earned. He was quite clear in his good-bye that he respected them too much to take advantage of them and sought rather to serve them. He made it plain that he did not ever take advantage of their hospitality nor did he consider himself above working with them. He states, "I have coveted no one's silver or gold or clothes. You yourselves know that these hands ministered to my own needs and to the men who were with me. In everything I showed you that by working hard in this manner you must help the weak and remember the words of the Lord Jesus, that He Himself said, 'It is more blessed to give than to receive'" (vv. 33–35). Paul, who should not have had to do this, defended his work ethic to this group and plainly preempted any accusation against his character in this regard. It is unfortunate, but many ministers today refuse to colabor with the congregation unless they have to. Paul set the opposite example and here reminded them that he earned his keep and covered expenses for his traveling companions as well. He was bivocational! He also noted that he did not desire any gifts from anyone but instead insisted on being the giver.

Many things have changed regarding the minister's work ethic and general approach to wealth since this speech was given. Without a doubt there was a day when ministers did all the work. Don't get me wrong, some still do. However, times have changed, and a new day has dawned. Gone are the old methods, strategies, and styles. There is nothing wrong with that, of course. But along with these "traditions," we've also lost a work ethic that we desperately need to get back. Ministers have slowly become identified by their speaking ability, their education, or their resume and not by their service to the congregation. So, they know what we have done and see what we do, but have no real idea of who we are. This problem is not just in the church, it is across the board. The generations of Buster, X and Y, have progressively become less loyal to institutions, less consistent with career choices, and less concerned about reputation. At the same time, we have become much more concerned with perception over reality. We live in a world where we don't know who we are, but we are clear that we do not want to do it like our parents and grandparents. Our culture, and its refusal to set boundaries, has happily obliged.

The work ethic in the church is defined by two extremes. There are those who do all the work because they are the victims of their own control issues and perfectionism. Then there are those that refuse to do anything but preach and pray because that is how they read Acts 6. It is clear that the Word and prayer are our primary ministries but are not our only ones. A simple reading of the rest of Acts shows that the apostles—especially Paul—were involved in so much more. In the postmodern era, I believe that we've overplayed our need to be with our family to the detriment of getting the work of the church done.[39] There is no doubt that family is more important than church, but I believe that both family time and church time are more important than "me time." In this individualistic society, many pastors have bought into the self-centeredness of "me focus." The ministry and the church have paid the price.

There is a balance to be reached that will win the respect of the congregation without placing upon oneself the angst of your children and wife. If you are called to do both, then do both! It really *is* that simple. Begin by first looking to identify with either extreme of workaholic or apathetic adolescent. We can go from there. A look at the biblical role of the pastor is essential to making this discussion objective, and an investigation of the most useful ministers in Scripture will make the expectation even more clear. Healthy churches are led by ministers whose minds are sharp, hearts are pure, and hands are dirty.

The Work Ethic of the Pastor

Before specific roles are identified for a pastor, a work ethic must be identified. Unfortunately, our work ethic is measured by Christ's! Jesus was simultaneously leader and servant. He gave attention and devotion to all that He was called to in both roles. Before pastors become pastors, they must be defined foundationally by Christ. Ministers are Christians, first and foremost. From this identity, all other responsibilities and callings must be birthed.

In Scripture, the pastor is called an overseer. The implication is both of responsibility and authority. By definition, this means that he carries the burdens of the body. This includes her health, calling, and task. As well, it also implies that if no one else is able or willing to take an essential role, often the responsibility falls on him. This is dysfunctional but necessary at times (especially within a small church). A healthy church needs an overseer who knows how to function in different roles, knows the people well, understands how to motivate them, and always keeps the Word and prayer as priorities in both personal life and church life. This cannot happen if he does everything himself or if he refuses to get his hands dirty in the intense labor of the ministry.

We've all been a part of churches that lack motivation and focus. Hopefully we've also been involved in churches where people cannot wait to go, are excited about ministry, love each other, share with the lost, and respect their leadership. With all churches being less than perfect, motivation does indeed become a great factor. However, there are a few rules that might help.

1. Do things that others consider important to church health, not just what you consider important. You are a community and God has placed you there because your total work effort is harmonious to Him. Make sure that you are working toward their personal goals and not just your own. This is how you discover group goals.

2. Give others the credit even if they don't completely deserve as much as you give. If they've played a role in ideas, planning, or working things through, recognize them.

3. Do not insist on getting recognized for what you do. God's future glory should suffice for us in this life. Refuse to play the numbers game with those in your church who are overfocused. Also, decline the numbers game with fellow pastors. Your faithful effort and that of the congregation is enough for God and should be enough for you as well.

4. Vehemently deny any accusations of laziness and passionately defend your work ethic. People will see that your work ethic and other people's perception of it are quite important. Paul would agree! Don't get bogged down in those who "tease"

about only working one day a week; rather, give focus to serious accusations against your character.

5. Give more weight to the opinions of people who have more "sweat equity" invested in a given area and let the congregation know that this is part of your methodology up front.

These key points are not without controversy and need more clarification and flexibility in application. "Should a minister ever stretch the truth?" "Should a person defend themselves against untruths?" "Shouldn't the minister lead the congregation and not the laity?" However, a meek, patient, kind, and Christ-like approach to motivating people is the best route to take. Consider the fact that Jesus allows us to be colaborers with Him! Mercy is a great act that God gives us and expects us to extend to others.

Paul told Timothy that a minister is called to be "above reproach," and this obviously includes his work ethic. Laziness is clearly a sin and is an affront to both God and His calling upon the minister's life. Note the Pauline Scriptures that reveal this reality.

- First Thessalonians 4:11–12 says that we must "work with our hands" as we lead a quiet life. This will win the respect of outsiders and makes us self-sufficient. Ephesians 4:28 makes a similar statement.
- Second Thessalonians 3:10–12 says point blank, "If a man will not work, he shall not eat." Then rebukes the lazy and says, "We command and urge in the Lord Jesus Christ to settle down and earn the bread they eat."

Solomon believed this to be something that his sons must grasp:

- Proverbs 28:19 states that "He who works his land will have abundant food, but the one who chases dreams will have his fill of poverty."

- Proverbs 13:4 states that the lazy person craves and gets nothing, but that the desires of the diligent are fully satisfied.
- Proverbs 10:4–5 points out that "lazy hands" make a man poor, but diligent hands bring wealth. Several other Proverbs make similar statements. See Proverbs 24:30–34 and Proverbs 12:11.
- Proverbs 20:13 speaks practical words of advice: "Do not love sleep or you will grow poor; stay awake and you will have food to spare."

It is quite clear that Solomon believed that the result of laziness was a field of thorns and a crop that was worthless. It is not fair to say that all dying churches are the result of laziness on the part of the minister. However, it is possible that our ministries are not producing fruit because we have insisted on only planting the seed through preaching and programs and have not watered, pulled weeds, nourished, and sheltered during the growing process.

Our Biblical Examples

How many of the great leaders of the faith were defined as those who knew how to delegate? How many revivals have arrived at the doorstep of churches that had ministers who spent all of their time in their studies with only personal study and prayer? God has always used those who understand that they were put on this earth to work hard and produce fruit for Him. How many of the parables dealt with labor? Jesus lived in a world of farms, vineyards, rented labor, slavery, wages, and expectation. He used the life staple of labor to make many points. However, the most important point He made about a divine work ethic was His own life. He offered everything and held nothing back. He healed, He taught, He challenged false teaching, He stood up for the downcast, He visited, He rebuked, He prayed, He fed, He carried, He walked miles upon miles. He was a very hard worker. And yet this did not hinder His own prayer life nor His preaching ministry.

Once again, think of the disciples after Jesus ascended. They saw His example and ran for the fields to harvest them. Nothing can be more laborious or more rewarding than harvest. The disciples understood that the whole concept of winning disciples, of fulfilling the Great Commission, was labor-intensive. Yet they ran to it, and in the end, most of them found their own deaths.

Paul is where we receive a great amount of our teaching on this subject. A minister is supposed to be a hard worker who knows how to prioritize and get things done. He, like Paul, is to pour himself out while understanding that some things can be delegated. Each ministry tells a story and models a work ethic. When people know you are a colaborer, they tend to not read into your absence and will readily defend you if you're unable to make it to the hospital. Human nature, however, does not easily forgive or forget laziness, nor should it. Lazy people have laid paths for destruction, fields of thorns, and lives of unproductivity.

Throughout Scripture, we find that every great leader is a great colaborer: Abraham, Isaac, Jacob, Joseph, Moses, David (except his one instance of laziness that cost him dearly), Jeremiah, Amos, Peter, Timothy, and many, many more. In Luke 11:42, Jesus rebuked the Pharisees for tithing but neglecting other righteous concepts that were more nebulous. They should have done both and so should we.

Conclusion: Heart and Hands

It is not by mistake or by passing remark that Paul makes this statement about being a colaborer among them in his final words to the Ephesian elders. It is also not just a statement about his "unlaziness." Note what a colaboring relationship with a congregation can bring with it.

1. A closer fellowship by actually spending quality one-on-one time with certain members or groups within the congrega-

tion. Staying in your study may bring you closer to God. It does not, however, draw you any closer to your congregation. Ministry with your congregants can do both. Neither should ever be seen as a substitution for the other.

2. Colaboring also develops a mutual respect within the church community. The minister's identity as "one of them" is essential. We seem to spend too much time expecting people to follow us because we hold a title and are less focused on giving them a reason to trust us.

3. Working with the congregation gives everyone ownership of the work. It is much harder to exit something that you've co-owned with the congregation and Christ.

4. Finally, colaboring gives a greater understanding for the pastor on what he's expecting of others. Oftentimes, our lives are centered around the church, and we expect others to live that way as well. We must not forget that this is our job, and they have their own jobs as well. If we are wearing ourselves out, we are wearing them out as well. Sensitivity goes a long way.

It could be that pastors are not close to our congregations for many different reasons. However, in my experience, this has been a significant cause for the distance between minister and congregation. It is not that the minister thinks himself better than the congregation, but it does appear that way for many people. This is an unfortunate reality in a society that does not like titles, authority structures, or a tier of leadership that leads to disconnection.

There is a serious struggle among American Evangelicals about the role of the pastor. We continually try to find a balance between the titles and stature of ministers. Much has changed in recent decades, and today's generation is not interested in such things. One thing that remains consistent is that we have made a false dichotomy between being a spiritual leader and being a colaborer. The two are not mutually exclusive. In fact, they are divinely connected.

We are taught by many experts to delegate, to train others, and to "work ourselves out of a job." What this translates to is that we only keep the jobs we like to do and with great hypocrisy, show frustration to church members that do the same thing. We must do the work of a pastor, evangelist, preacher, and overseer and remember to use our other gifts and skills within the church at large. As I often remind my students (and myself), we are not just called to work where we are gifted, but we are equally called to where we are needed.

This struggle between the extreme-delegating pastor and the colaboring pastor is brilliantly and comically shared in Calvin Miller's *O Shepherd, Where art Thou?*[40] This book tells the tale of a pastor who wants to work himself out of a job as he is taught by his spiritual hero but is "haunted" at the same time by the ghost of Richard Baxter, the great minister who wrote *The Reformed Pastor*.[41] *O Shepherd* points out that, in many cases, we have to make a decision if we want to be a minister that meets society's expectations or one that meets the shepherding needs of God's people. Somewhere along the line, we have falsely determined that if a church is large enough, the pastor can let someone else do his job. Granted, the larger the church, the greater the responsibilities. Even so, pastors can't let go of the foundational call of leading people into a mature faith in Christ. This takes personal attention.

Baxter's brilliant and timeless work is a must-read for all ministers. He reminds us of simpler times when ministers knew the people in the congregation and when they knew who their unsaved family members were. Everyone had access to the pastor, but more importantly, the pastor had access to the people. Preaching and administrating are indeed important tasks. However, we cannot lose sight of the role of the pastor to pray with the sick, to visit those who are in prison or shut in to their homes. Pastors have the privilege of coming in to the most personally sacred of places on this earth—homes, hospital rooms, waiting rooms, dining rooms, funeral parlors, and many more. Don't lose sight of these callings as both a gift and a privilege. Erwin McManus writes, "The life of the church is the heart of God. The heart of God is to serve a broken world…the serving we are called to requires direct contact. You cannot wash the feet of the dirty world if you refuse to touch it."[42] While our avoidance of dirty work may be normal in our context, it has been a longstanding tradition of great churches and their ministers to get themselves quite dirty.

Labor is good. It is one of the many things that we were put on this earth to do. Notice what the preacher says in Ecclesiastes.

> Then I realized that it is good and proper for a man to eat and drink, and to find satisfaction in his toilsome labor under the sun during the few days of life God has given him—for this is his lot. Moreover, when God gives any man wealth and possessions, and enables him to enjoy them, to accept his lot and be happy in his work—this is a gift of God. (Ecclesiastes 5:18–19).

Did you see that? A gift from God! That is what our labor is. It gives us confidence, identity, purpose, satisfaction, credibility, and much, much more. God has offered us the opportunity to laugh, weep, and rejoice with our congregations. We must not forget that he's also given us the opportunity to sweat, strain, and wear ourselves out with them as well! This is the foundation of true fellowship.

8

Open Your Heart to Them (Acts 20:36–38)

The conclusion of Paul's Miletus speech is one of the most emotionally moving moments of any biblical narrative. Luke describes the heartrending scenario.

> When he had said these things, he knelt down and prayed with them all. And they began to weep aloud and embraced Paul, and repeatedly kissed him, grieving especially over the word which he had spoken, that they would not see his face again. And they were accompanying him to the ship. (Acts 20:36–38)

This scene says a lot! It reveals truths about the relationship between Paul and the Ephesian elders. It gives us a glimpse in to the meaningful ministry that took place among them, and it shows what type of tears *should* accompany an exit. Notice how it ends: communication, prayer, embracing, affection, grief, and an extended good-bye all the way to the ship! How many ministers' relocations have a sendoff like this?

The end of a ministry should be tearful, but not tears of anger, frustration, or regret, but rather tears of love and sorrow. It is rather clear that Paul earned such a farewell. It is something that we have to work for as well. Looking at the details of the ministry that Paul has spelled out so far in his Miletus address, it is plain to see that such a good-bye was to be expected. They were family and no one wants to let family go, especially when they know it is the last time they will see each other.

If the apostle Paul had to work for this type of relationship, it stands to reason that we will have to work hard and long to achieve such results. Although not comprehensive, we can gather basic concepts and steps that we can take as pastors to build such a fellowship of spiritual intimacy. No other leadership profession has the potential for such a powerful bond between the leader and any given group of people. The following ideas will give a general direction toward achieving such a goal.

The first step is to model an attitude of vulnerability. Have you ever noticed that it was the legalistic, pompous Pharisees and Scribes and the theologically liberal Sadducees that felt uncomfortable around Jesus? Everyone else was able to know Him, approach Him, and even speak to Him about their questions, their needs, and about life. He did have a core group of disciples, and the inner three, but He made time for people. He was with them. Jesus's name was "God with us." This defined a major part of His ministry.

Again, have you ever thought about how difficult it would be to make yourself vulnerable to the affections, deceptions, and schemes of people when you were God and knew exactly what they were going to do? And yet Jesus loved Judas, treated Him as a friend, let him be the treasurer, and never lost His temper with his money-obsessed questions. What about tolerating Peter's high view of himself and his insistence on answering every question before anyone else? Jesus knew that Peter would flunk the ultimate test three times in a matter of hours. "You were one of them, weren't you?" Yet, Jesus encouraged him, let him into the "inner three," and even washed his feet.

We are only going to make a difference in people's lives if we are determined to take them at their word and at their intentions and refuse to read into the situation of what might happen, what scheme they might be working on, and whether or not they are out to get us! It is a difficult balance, I admit. However, Jesus was able to protect the unity of the disciples while allowing them all to scatter from Him in His greatest hour of need. That is a vulnerability that most ministers would refuse to demonstrate. We are too protective, too sensitive, and too proud. In this way, we are not much like Jesus at all. He was vulnerable toward people He couldn't trust. Are we?

The next step is to demonstrate genuine trust. Do you trust your congregation? How much? Would you allow church members to use their gifts without micromanaging them? Would you allow them to present ideas to the church without you approving every aspect of the program? Do you trust that the vote will go well because God is in this motion? Would you trust them with the truth? With taking care of your family if you were gone? With your life?

Your congregation knows whether or not you trust them. So does your staff and deacons. If you are not willing to sleep and let them keep watch, take a break, and let them preach or let someone else chair the committee, then you don't trust them, and they (and everyone else) know it. Think for a minute about the sleeping disciples. Jesus trusted them to "watch and pray," and they failed Him. More than once! Yet He gave them trust each time. Jesus trusted the disciples with the "inside information" of the Gospel, knowing that they would scatter when he died. How deep does your trust go?

A noticeable differentiation must be made between trusting people and trusting God to work through them. No one is completely trustworthy, but everyone has the opportunity to allow God to work through them in amazing ways. We must be careful about not crossing the line between being realistic about them and being skeptical of God's ability to change them. I know that a balance must be in place, but too many congregants feel like their pastor does not trust them. I hope they are not ours.

Third, ministers must be open and honest. This seems obvious since the Bible talks of Jesus as "The Truth" and our adversary as the "father of lies." However, if we are honest, we will admit that being honest with people is hard to do. No one wants to hear the truth when it is discouraging or when it has the potential to wreck our plans, hopes, and dreams. However, a pastor must express himself in an honest way, with a gentleness that gives evidence to the Spirit's fruit in his life. If the members of a church believe their pastor to be more interested in avoiding conflict than in being honest, it will speak to the overall character of the minister, and the church will suffer.

Your congregation should be able to trust you and take you at your word. When they ask for your advice, give it to them. Explain yourself and support them in any way that you can. Genuineness is clearly lacking in postmodern America. People are looking for it and should be able to find it in the church. It is our job to make sure they can.

Some practical ways to demonstrate openness with your congregation is to allow them to see inside of your plans, dreams, and hopes. No doubt, there are opinions that you can definitely keep to yourself, but who you really are must come out in your preaching, counseling, and ministering. Too many ministers are not trusted by the people they are called to lead because they are perceived as being distant. If we preach the truth, they trust our theology. If we guide them in the truth, they trust our leadership. Letting them see who you really are as a person is the kind of honesty they need from you to truly know you and trust you rather than just trusting certain things you do. At that point, they will open their lives up to you as well.

Fourth, you should share your life and your family's life with them. Along with the advice to be open and honest, we must make sure that we are not too protective of our families. I've heard many "experts" say and write that we must protect our family from certain things in the church. This is not a bad idea in and of itself. Nonetheless, ministers have taken it too far in many instances and do not allow the congregation to welcome us as a part of the family. In turn, both our congregation and our wives and children subliminally conclude that the other is not worth really knowing.

The more you can share about your family's tragedies and triumphs, about your joys and pains, your dreams and your fears, the closer you are to them as a unit and the more empowered you are to minister in their homes and them in yours. Ministers must work toward the kind of unity that they expect from others. If we are to be a family and are to be smaller parts fit in to a whole, the pastor's family must be the first to demonstrate this.

Next, ministers must be careful not to be overly suspicious of church member's motives. Not everyone is out to get you! We sometimes act as though this is true, especially when we've been hurt before. It is a rare circumstance, but some ministers seem to be paranoid about certain people and/or segments within the church. It is understandable to be guarded with those who have proven to have less-pure motives and methods. Even so, we cannot carry on any ministry with suspicion. It will go nowhere.

Perhaps one of the saddest statements I heard while visiting with a staff member revealed some very bitter feelings toward the congregation. I had gotten to know some of the members of that particular church, and I stated to the staff member that there were a lot of really good people here. The quick response was, "I wouldn't really say 'a lot.'" The sentiment struck me to the core, but I realized I had felt that way before as well. In many circumstances we have earned the right to be bitter by the world's standards. We've had salaries cut, been yelled at, been accused, lied to, misquoted, and purposefully misunderstood. We have had folks question our integrity, our family, our work ethic, our intelligence, and our motives. Indeed, the world would give us a free pass to be bitter, even unforgiving and spiteful. However, we do not live by the world's standards. Jesus alone has the right to be bitter. We may have the right to be hurt, frustrated, or exhausted, but not bitter. We are required to forgive them, trust their motives, and love them unconditionally.

Finally, make sure to start each ministry without baggage. It is a common occurrence that in today's divorce-ridden society, a second marriage is plagued by the problems of the first. The lack of trust, the hurt of abuse, the pain of neglect, and the emptiness of failure represent some of the baggage that we can carry with us from one relationship to another. It is quite common in the pastor-church relationship as well. Churches and ministers need a fresh start. They need to work toward healing, forgiveness, and health.

We often live by the motto, "Fool me once, shame on you…fool me twice, shame on me!" This may have a lot to say about worldly wisdom, but shows little resemblance to the Christian standard of forgiven sinners. We, as ministers, should work to protect our families and sometimes ourselves from needless pain. However, we cannot allow these self-preservation instincts to be our default approach in all situations, especially in new contexts. Perhaps faith in God to provide protection for you and your family will take away some of the burden, allowing you to give a new situation a new opportunity.

Wouldn't it be nice if there was not any baggage to carry? This, of course, is the point of this book and the "moral" of the story in regard to ministerial resignations. If we would make sure that we've accomplished what we were called to do, we could find our new place of ministry an unwritten story of God's soon-revealed greatness.

Love Never Fails

People who speak, sing, or dream of love as a natural and easy thing may be missing something! How hard is it to really love someone the way that God expects us to? How hard is it to give what 1 Corinthians 13 describes to someone to whom you are not related? We learn a lot from reading the Gospels in this regard. Jesus demonstrated love in perfect balance with everything else. It was natural for Him because He was perfect, but it was not cheap or easy—it cost Him everything. We must discipline ourselves to love each other, and we are expected to take it as far as loving our own personal enemies. There is no other path toward godliness than to love in a way that the world is made aware of who we are. To this discussion, we will now give focus.

God could have "thrown down the gauntlet" on any virtue or moral command that he desired. He can demand from people what he wants and can bless or judge how He sees fit. He is in complete control. It is all about Him, and the sky is the limit (and then some)! However, it was *love* that God chose to elevate above all other virtues and offerings (1 Corinthians 13). It was love that is promised to never fail us (1 Corinthians 13:13). It was love that God chose to show to sinners (Romans 5:8) and demanded that we give to Him (Luke 10:27), our neighbors (Luke 10:27b), and even our enemies (Matthew 5:44)!

Love and God go together. It was love that God gave to "thousands" (Deuteronomy 5:10), and it was His love that we are promised will always be available to His children (Romans 8:35–39). Finally, when given one word to describe God, John the Elder (Jesus's best friend on earth) used the description of love (1 John 4:8). It is clear that love is nonnegotiable, and God has high expectations that our love for Him is always connected with obedience.

God's love is found through sacrifice resulting in reconciliation. Jesus demonstrated this, explained this, and expects this of those who desire to follow Him. Our denial of self-love and our consideration of others as more important than we are is a mandatory conviction of discipleship (Philippians 2:3). Without unity we've failed at our second greatest commandment, and we've hindered the lost from knowing the God-sent Christ (John 13:35). Our unity is required for the growth and health of our congregation. Genuinely loving one another is our method toward reaching the world.

Earning a Heartfelt Good-bye

Paul shows us that a ministerial exit can be emotional but also rewarding. Note the elements of this farewell. First, after praying, they wept. Second, they embraced one another. Third, they kissed him. Finally, they grieved his exit, especially that he had informed them that this was the last time they would see his face. After the good-bye, they followed him to the ship. What an emotional, intimate, and personal farewell!

Everyone's hearts were broken because everyone's hearts were open. Scripture expects this of our ministries. No one stumbles upon a good-bye like this—it is earned through the elements we've already discussed so far. The lessons that we've investigated from Paul's ministry to the Ephesians are summed up in this chapter's exhortation, to love your people sincerely and deeply. Paul had opened up his heart to the Ephesians, and they responded. He was loved and trusted by them because he loved and trusted them first.

Once again, we see plainly throughout Scripture that God uses men who have open hearts toward their congregation. We have Christ's example, the Holy Spirit's fruit, and Paul's many exhortations that emphasize love, kindness, trust, and perseverance through relational difficulties and forgiveness when wronged. When we truly love our congregation like family, we love the senior adults as grandparents and parents, peers as your brothers, and their children as our own. We will definitely hug, cry, share, and laugh together on a level seen in few functional families in postmodern America. Ministry is not just about sharing Scripture, time, and fellowship, it is about sharing lives like Christ shared His.

This affection in the church was not exclusive to the Ephesians. Note what he says to the church at Philippi, "For God is my witness, how I long for you all with the affection of Christ Jesus" (Philippians 1:8), and to the Thessalonian congregation, "Having so fond an affection for you, we were well-pleased to impart to you not only the Gospel of God but also our own lives, because you had become very dear to us" (1 Thessalonians 2:8). We've seen throughout this study that Paul loved them and wanted them to be aware of his affection. We must learn from Paul.

In the coming chapters, we will see a reiteration of what Paul had stated to the Ephesian elders as he instructs young pastor Timothy in the specifics of being a pastor. Paul had an open-heart policy. He took the lead from Jesus on this one and so should we! If we love deeply, sincerely, affectionately, and in the Spirit of

Christ, that love will return upon us, granting us a fond farewell of bittersweet memories overwhelmed by a confidence that God is at the heart of the separation. We then say good-bye just as we've lived, ministered, and grown in faith and love.

Selah: Truly Understanding Where You Are

We are now at a very important part of the process, moving from evaluation toward problem solving. I do not believe this to be an illogical or premature leap by any means, but that does not necessarily make the mental or spiritual transition easy. There is still much left to think about, to meditate on, to pray over, to converse with your wife and mentor, and to hash out with God. I pray that the following chapters will be beneficial to you, but you need to be ready for them. Perhaps you read them now and reread them again once you are ready for it. But this chapter is a bit of a transition, if you will. A pause, or *selah*.

The term *selah* is found scattered throughout David's Psalms. It, in essence, is a term that gives direction to the musicians who are playing along. It is a command to stop, pause, and consider what has just been said. Some of the greatest lines in David's writings are followed with this musical direction. Some are quite pertinent to where you are right now:

- Psalm 4:4. Tremble, and do not sin; Meditate in your heart upon your bed, and be still. Selah.

- Psalm 24:6. This is the generation of those who seek Him, Who seek Your face—*even* Jacob. Selah.

- Psalm 32:7. You are my hiding place; You preserve me from trouble; You surround me with songs of deliverance. Selah.

- Psalm 52:3. You love evil more than good, Falsehood more than speaking what is right. Selah.

- Psalm 61:4. Let me dwell in Your tent forever; Let me take refuge in the shelter of Your wings. Selah.

- Psalm 62:8. Trust in Him at all times, O people; Pour out your heart before Him; God is a refuge for us. Selah.

There is so much to consider, so many thoughts that need to percolate, so many truths that need to be deeply pondered. However, one Psalm, a Psalm of Asaph that is most pertinent for this discussion is Psalm 77.

> My voice rises to God, and He will hear me. In the day of my trouble I sought the Lord; In the night my hand was stretched out without weariness; My soul refused to be comforted. When I remember God, then I am disturbed; When I sigh, then my spirit grows faint. Selah. You have held my eyelids open; I am so troubled that I cannot speak. I have considered the days of old, The years of long ago. I will remember my song in the night; I will meditate with my heart, And my spirit ponders: Will the Lord reject forever? And will He never be favorable again? Has His loving kindness ceased forever? Has His promise come to an end forever? Has God forgotten to be gracious, Or has He in anger withdrawn His compassion? Selah. Then I said, 'It is my grief, That the right hand of the Most High has changed.' I shall remember the deeds of the lord; Surely I will remember Your wonders of old. I will meditate on all Your work And muse on Your deeds. Your way, O God, is holy; What god is great like our God? You are the God who works wonders; You have made known Your strength among the peoples. You have by Your power redeemed Your people, The sons of Jacob and Joseph. Selah. The waters saw You, O God; The waters saw You, they were in anguish; The deeps also trembled. The clouds poured out water; The skies gave forth a sound; Your arrows flashed here and there. The sound of Your thunder was in the whirlwind; The lightnings lit up the world; The earth trembled and shook. Your way was in the sea And Your paths in the mighty waters, And Your footprints may not be known. You led Your people like a flock By the hand of Moses and Aaron.' (Psalm 77:1–20)

To me, it has always been amazing how honest the psalmists felt they could be with God about frustrations and disappointments. It is quite unfortunate that most questions aimed at God are those from the lips of immature believers. I would imagine that at times they seem quite shrill to the ears of the Father. In contrast, however, are the prayers of despair from the heart of mature believers struggling with this world in the same manner that God struggles with this world. They are disillusioned with the lack of love, vision, and hunger for the things of God. They are brokenhearted over the things that break God's heart as well. They are tired of politics, business meetings, accusations, and dissensions. These prayers have depth. They have substance, and they are profound. We pray them and then we ponder them. We share our pain and frustration, but we also express our faith and hope. If you are toward the end of your prayer and ready to consider the hope that lies ahead and can see that a new day is about to arrive, then you are ready for the remainder of this book. However, if you are still in the "early verses" of Psalm 77, there are some things for you to consider.

Transitioning

As earlier mentioned, perceived failure in the ministry is more complex than it is in any other area of life. Albeit strange, it is one of the few professions that one can love and hate at the same time. We love it for what it is supposed to be and despise it for what it often becomes. With this stress comes pain on several levels: spiritual, mental, physical, and emotional. With this in mind, there are a handful of things to consider.

1. A "bad" ministry (one where nothing goes right) does not equate a failure in your calling nor does it serve as a barometer for future ministries.

2. Careful evaluation of what caused the problems is essential. It could be mistakes that you've committed, it could have nothing to do with you. However, it is important to know,

to the best of your ability, what actually has happened. If it can be dealt with, do so biblically and in a spirit of Christ.

3. All ministers fail (and I do mean all!). We are sinners placed in an eternally important position. However, all people in all professions fail—business, academia, entertainment, and athletics just to name a few. There are many more people in this world that go unknown, unnoticed, and underappreciated than there are who become famous. Remember, fame can be brought upon a person by their ability, by chance, or by their mistakes.

4. God has been and will always be a healer. He is Yahweh-Rapha who heals. He expressed Himself in Christ as the physician that came for the sick. If you are ill, then He is ready to heal. He enjoys doing this if we will allow Him the opportunity.

5. Be patient, humble, kind, and self-disciplined. Just being godly can be enough to get us through these tumultuous rides at times. However, the Fruit of the Spirit is always the right response. If we wait, we mount up like eagles and find strength beyond ourselves. It should be pointed out that the number of days, months, or even years is never equivalent to waiting or being patient. The intention is not that you tried to last as long as you could, but that you were patient. Success in this area is staying until God moves you.

6. Anchor deep. Find the rock of our Lord sufficient. Cling to Him through His Word, prayer, and worship. As well, find friends, mentors, and family members that can walk through this process with you. I would avoid anyone from within the body, this can cause dissention whether you stay or go. Reach out to colleagues, local professors at the Bible college, seminary or fellow pastors, denominational employees, and the like. They can give you perspective that you do not currently have. You can learn from their wisdom and from their mistakes as well.

7. Know that Christ suffered for you and He called you well aware that these days would come. He has already identified with your suffering so that you could fellowship with Him in yours (Philippians 3:10).

In the chapters to follow, I have made assumptions about your willingness to "stay on in Ephesus." I pray that this is your wish. If not, I pray that you will have an honest take on what has happened, how it happened, and why it happened and will take the lessons learned with you. I completely understand when the minister's hands are tied and they are forced to leave, either in a vocal or nonverbal manner. However, if there are folks who are still ready to follow you, dreams that you would leave unfulfilled, missions not embarked on, and plans still not seen through, I pray that you will give it one more try and find that His grace will once again be sufficient.

When counseling couples who are considering divorce, we pastors always look for the hope of a healthy marriage in the future even if the couple cannot see it. The avenue to that dream includes: forgiveness, honesty, patience, expressive love, and God's constant assistance. The formula for our minister-church reconciliation is not much different. In most cases, I see a great ministry, a genuine healing, and much fruit. You may be the rare exception to this possibility, but do not assume this to be true simply because it feels true. I challenge you to read on and take a step of faith.

PART 3

Strategies in Moving Forward

9

Heed Paul's Pastoral Advice
(1 and 2 Timothy)

It is quite interesting and divinely mysterious how God ordained the local church to function. Many different peoples, cultures, and nationalities have constructed what they believe to be the best form of local church government. Whether it be governed by a pastor, a board, a council, an entire congregation, or things are managed by a denomination, the reality that sinful humans are intimately involved in the direction and priorities of churches is a given. Even so, God has given us the opportunity for success through revealing His will regarding church management. We have one of the clearest set of ministerial instructions in Paul's letter to Timothy.

What we find in 1 and 2 Timothy is immensely helpful to our search for meaning and direction in a struggling church. In these letters we see a real minister with real problems getting real advice! By giving his protégé a lifeline, Paul also gives us a very personal relationship letter where more specifics are given regarding church ministry, church structure, and church management than anywhere else in Scripture. It is noteworthy how consistent Paul is in what he did in his own ministry, what he claimed to the Ephesian elders about his ministry, and what he expects of others, namely Timothy and us. Through these various venues, we see three versions of the same story!

Pastor Timothy

Scripture offers some background about this young pastor that allows us to identify with him more closely. First, Timothy's family served as anchors to his faith as both his mother and grandmother were women of strong faith (2 Timothy 1:5) who trained Timothy in the Word (2 Timothy 3:15). Second, Timothy would have had some cultural identity issues having a Jewish mother and a Gentile father. This would have made him both appealing to people like him but also he would have been rejected by both Jews and Gentiles who did not understand the far-reaching implications of the Gospel of unity. Third, Timothy knew that he needed a mentor. He happened to have a very able one! Paul himself circumcised Timothy and invited him to be a traveling companion to several cities. As he grew in the faith, Paul sent Timothy on his own behalf to serve. The most notable of these churches are Philippi and Corinth. This commissioning leads us to a fourth point that Timothy needed lots of training before he was ready to pastor on his own. Clearly, Paul was intent on training Timothy for the ministry and, therefore, spent a great amount of time with him. Notably, Timothy is mentioned as being with Paul while at least six of the biblical Epistles were penned. He served as well as a traveling companion of Silas and was very highly respected among the early church. Finally, Timothy had to have tough skin because he suffered a lot.

Although church tradition varies on specifics, Timothy most likely served as pastor of Ephesus for approximately fifteen years. Early tradition claims he was martyred in the city for the preaching he did against idols on behalf of the Gospel. Hopefully, like Timothy, we can also claim one final similarity as Timothy remains one of the untarnished figures in church history that have been well-respected and admired throughout the history of the church.

As we put ourselves in Timothy's shoes, remember that this letter is intended to be both instructive and encouraging. It is quite clear that Paul thought Timothy to be highly qualified and very competent for this job. He is not trying to save a fledgling ministry or minister, but is rather giving insight to someone who desperately needs it. The two epistles should be received with the same spirit today. What we have, in essence, are the basic rules of pastoral ministry.

Basic Rules of the Pastoral Ministry

The basic purpose of these letters, as explained by Chrysostom, was to challenge Timothy to be a genuine Christian by fighting heresy while at the same time promoting the Gospel in speech and life.[43] Under these broad themes, several subthemes can be found. It is here that Paul shares his "insider information" from apostle to pastor regarding the manner in which one must conduct a ministry that will begin and end well. Without a doubt, there is an undeniable love from Paul, not only for Timothy and the church but also for the pastorate as well. The position itself is a privilege and is more than worth the effort that it requires. Paul describes it as a "fine work" (1 Timothy 3:1) and limits such a role through certain requirements. As a highly viewed calling, it has never been a job that just anyone could do. Being a good pastor doesn't come naturally, no matter how gifted one is for the office or how called one feels toward the service. Paul informs Timothy that being a pastor is a spiritual job above and beyond any natural ability that one might possess, and there is very little that one could ever consider natural about it. No one was born with the "knack" for pastoring. We, as born sinners, were born to fail in the ministry! Our sinful nature wants the very opposite of serving, sacrificing, and perhaps suffering. Paul gives a path toward success, and there are no other avenues.

1. *Love as an attitude, action, and foundation.* Once again, we see that everything for Paul was grounded in love. Agape was the

eternal gift that held the church together (1 Corinthians 13) and the first mentioned fruit of the Holy Spirit (Galatians 5). Jesus had identified it as the telltale sign of His church, and Paul concluded that it was the one thing that we actually "owed" to one another (Galatians 5:13). Therefore, it comes as no surprise that early on, Paul sets it as the most important goal of ministry by stating in 1 Timothy 1:5, "But the goal of our instruction is love from a pure heart and a good conscience and a sincere faith." "Paul is specifically giving the reason for Timothy's involvement, namely, to arouse the love which comes from a pure heart. The false teachers are involved in speculations (v. 4) and meaningless talk (v. 6) that are full of deception (4:1–2) and lead to quarrels and suspicions (6:4–5). The purpose in ordering them to stop is to bring the church back to the proper result…their loving of one another."[44] A ministry without a genuine, covenantal commitment as a goal is oxymoronic and counterproductive. By establishing agape as both the foundation and goal for the pastoral ministry, Paul's advice that is given is timeless in nature.

2. *Work through your problems.* At the very beginning of his letter, Pastor Timothy is encouraged to *stay on in Ephesus* even though things were rough. Ephesus was a very difficult place to do ministry. The dynamics of the city included overindulgence, a transient and disconnected population, sensuality, extreme individuality, and a spiritual overemphasis. The issues for Timothy were not much different than it is for us in postmodern America. Clearly, it is during these times that bold but patient leadership is needed. Paul instructed Timothy that suffering and pain are a natural part of the ministry and consistently accepted this reality himself.

    This command is much more than a rousing halftime speech. Staying on in Ephesus was fundamental to God's purpose for both Timothy and the Ephesians church.

Scripture makes it clear in Philippians 3:10 that our suffering glorifies God and allows us the privilege of fellowship with the suffering Christ.

There is also a very practical reason why Paul refused to let Timothy give up. In 2 Timothy 2:10–13, Paul notes that Timothy's hardships are to be endured for the sake of the *elect*. Paul is saying,

> There are those in your congregation who get it, Timothy, and they are worth the attacks you receive and the sacrifices that you are making. They were worthy of Christ's sacrifice and elected to receive God's grace. God has chosen you to lead them. They are of high value and your pain is worth their spiritual health.

Paul knew Timothy had not yet reached his time of resignation. Chances are, it was something that Timothy had already known as well.

3. *Be a Theologian on offense.* Paul also charged Timothy to *defend orthodoxy and keep the doctrine of the Christian church pure.* This charge is repeated early and often in both epistles. On the opposite end of things, heretical teachings are addressed throughout both letters as well. Timothy was expected to be an example, to be strong and sober, to teach truth, and to combat false teachings and false teachers. However, the issue was even more complex than that. While Timothy needed to lead the church to reject heresy, the church was not interested in orthodoxy (1 Timothy 1:3–4). Does this sound familiar? He definitely had his work cut out for him! What they wanted was to have their "ears tickled" and their own views confirmed, but he was called to bring them what God wanted them to have, not what they desired to hear.

It is essential to note that we do not know all the details about what type of heresies were being taught. Of course, we know that common heresies included attacks on the Trinity, on the divinity of Christ, the path to salvation, the promotion of Gnosticism, and the allowance of an immoral life. Few specifics are offered describing what Timothy was facing. However, it is clear that Paul trusted that Timothy would understand. As well, I believe that we understand clearly as well.

There were a few employable methods to lead to orthodoxy. Timothy is reminded in 1 Timothy 4:13c. There Paul encourages, "Until I come, give attention to the *public reading of Scripture*, to exhortation and teaching." He is also instructed to "Pay close attention to yourself and to your teaching; persevere in these things, for as you do this you will ensure salvation both for yourself and for those who hear you."[45] What is on the line in regard to biblical doctrine is nothing less than the salvation of souls, the health of Christ's bride, and the truth of the Gospel. The final expectation of orthodoxy was given in 2 Timothy where Paul pleads,

> O Timothy, guard what has been entrusted to you, avoiding worldly *and* empty chatter *and* the opposing arguments of what is falsely called "knowledge"—which some have professed and thus gone astray from the faith. Grace be with you.

Without orthodoxy, growth will only be dysfunctional and, in the end, destructive.

4. *Contentment comes through God.* The next guideline given for the pastorate was that he should not desire what he did not have: wealth, more years of experience, different congregants, a different town to call home, etc. This remains especially true today in every way. Recall that Paul made it plain in the Miletus speech that he worked hard and did not covet anyone's wealth (Acts 20:33–35). As well, he encourages Timothy to take a similar position of working hard and being content with what you've been given even

if the church seems to be falling apart and you are ready to call it quits.

In my experience, I've found that the people who are most obsessed with money are not the wealthy, but rather the poor or struggling. People who have money realize that it does not hold any secret power or grant any special peace. However, people of lesser means often believe that it does. In all honesty, compensation is a huge reason for ministerial unhappiness in America. However, one's calling must trump their compensation. The commandment to not love money needs no further explanation. Wealth is the enemy of humility because money feeds pride and indulges lusts. The same is especially true for the pastor. Jesus Himself said you cannot love God and money at the same time (Matthew 6:24).

Many ministries have been destroyed due to the love of money and most of these are not Bakers and Swaggarts who are wealthy. Indeed many decisions of calling to and ministry within a given setting are based on money or the lack thereof. Although it is difficult for ministers to take fiscal risks with children, much can be learned through raising a family on limited means and depending on the generosity of God's people to meet your needs. Trusting God with provision is an ancient calling of God's people and it has never failed to pay dividends! David noted in Psalm 37:25 that he had never seen the "righteous forsaken or their descendants begging for bread." Of course that doesn't mean there are not righteous people who have very limited resources, it is more that David had never seen them have to beg. Our wealth is God's decision. He alone is our provider.

Although some who have wrongly joined capitalism and Christianity too closely might disagree, Paul is clearly stating that desiring wealth and desiring the ministry are mutually exclusive aspirations. Wealth and service are most likely going to be two separate options in this world. Of course, in postmodern America, everyone is wealthy to some degree. However, opulence is cautioned, especially for one who is called to wash feet for a living (1 Timothy 6:6–10; 2 Timothy 3:3). Can a minister of the Gospel be wealthy? Yes, of course. Is this a probability? I would say not in most situations. If you do gain wealth, then generosity, stewardship, and humility must accompany it. The same is true for those who have much less.

5. *Hold yourself to God's standards of polity.* The fifth pastoral exhortation is quite simple, the pastor is to *promote what God expects of the church*, particularly qualifications for the ministers. Ministry is service to God and His will first and then to the people. If one wishes to be successful in God's eyes, they must be committed to divine qualifications. Overseers and deacons are set apart and their qualifications require something more than simple Christian living. Jesus's call to ministers is one of moral purity. The idea is for them to be above reproach or accusation.

Along with personnel, God's methodology must be utilized in dealing with the culture (1 Timothy 3:1–7), the use of God's Word, and the handling of debates (1 Timothy 6:3–5), the temptation to be partial toward certain members (1 Timothy 5:20–21), and in dealing with apostasy (1 Timothy 4:1ff). As well, Paul offers some advice regarding women and their role in the church. These teachings make it clear that God does have an opinion on every essential matter within the church and that it is His opinion alone that matters.

6. *Intercede for others.* Another fundamental of the pastoral ministry is prayer. Communication with God on a regular basis and in a humble manner is mandatory for effective service. This should come as no surprise to any minister. Specifically, Paul encouraged intercession for others, "Therefore I want the men in every place to pray, lifting

up holy hands, without wrath and dissension" in 1 Timothy 2:1–8. Timothy was asked to pray for all men, for kings, and all who are in authority. However, it is quite obvious that this command is meant to cover the gamut of prayer for the entire Christian life. People everywhere are to do it and to pray in a manner that is both noticeable and humble.

A minister must have a healthy prayer life. This is a given for all believers. However, a healthy prayer life of intercession is a requirement for ministers, and it is not just for specific people, but for all people. Intercessory prayer draws the pastor closer to God and to the congregation and is another avenue that God has put in place to make the fellowship and the minister stronger. Timothy had a lot of people working against him. However, praying for them was as essential as correcting them.

7. *Preaching is still primary.* Finally, an overseer is to preach the Word. This mandate is the heart of 2 Timothy. There are three key points about the type of preaching that the young pastor is expected to practice. First, it is to be biblical since the Scriptures are God-breathed (2 Timothy 3:16–17). This mandate seems logical and simple. However, many sermons throughout church history have been anything but biblical. It must be Scripture-driven, not needs-driven. The Bible does not need to be made relevant, it is! Next, the preaching of the Word is to be done whether it is being received or not. It is to be conducted with boldness and authority and without apology even if no one seems to be listening to it. Paul refers to these times of growth and drought as seasons. The preaching of God's Word is always right in His time regardless of whether or not it is being openly received by people. Finally, the Word is to be proclaimed in a manner that teaches orthodox doctrine, trains the people for ministry, and reminds them of God's will for the church. Paul refers to this method as "rightly dividing the Word" in 2 Timothy 2:15. Much of what is considered great preaching

relies heavily on emotion and passion. This has been a sad reality for quite some time. With this in mind, Spurgeon encouraged his students to set a different standard.

> Sermons should have real teaching in them, and their doctrine should be solid, substantial, and abundant. We do not enter the pulpit to talk for talk's sake; we have instructions to convey, important to the last degree, and we cannot afford to utter pretty nothings. Our range of subjects is all but boundless, and we cannot, therefore, be excused if our discourses are threadbare and devoid of substance.[46]

Clearly, it is not simply passion, zeal, and clear speech that makes a church healthy, it is doing the more difficult work of exegesis, study, and application that makes a body healthy. Paul wanted Timothy's preaching to give the congregation confidence in their faith, assurance in their struggles, and equip them to do the work of Christ's Kingdom. As well, it strengthened his own faith, solidified his doctrine, and challenged his convictions.

Conclusion

What Paul told Timothy is timeless on so many levels. Paul both desired and expected his son Timothy to be effective in the ministry that God had called him to even though ministry was tough. Timothy's mentor hoped that the young pastor would be bold yet thoughtful, empowered by the Spirit yet weak before the throne. He aimed at producing a minister that proclaimed a Word that touched his heart before he intended it to change others. The pastor, in Paul's estimation, was to be identified not by numbers nor by recommendations or accolades. Rather, a biblical pastor was to be synonymous with genuineness, humility, reverence, patience, and was to be inspiring to his congregation and a sweet aroma to his God. Nothing less would do in a first-century church. Nothing less will do for a twenty-first-century church either.

10

Pray Effectively for a Healthy Church

The value of prayer is impossible to overestimate. Without a healthy prayer life, we as ministers are sunk and the church has no future. The greatness of a person, family, church, or nation is defined fundamentally by prayer. Some may disagree, but Moses would beg to differ! He believed that we must view greatness through the lens of the truth as stated in Deuteronomy 4:7. Here, Moses defines human stature as a measure of God's willingness to talk to us; both through His law (or now the Bible) and prayer. "For what great nation is there that has a god so near to it as is the lord our God whenever we call on Him?" Prayer is God saying loud and clear that He wants to be a part of our lives and desires for us to find our ultimate purpose serving Him. No greater words of self-worth could be offered by our Creator! Prayer is crucial to all of our decisions in ministry, including whether or not it is time to go. However, prayer must be biblically informed if it is to be eternally significant.

Prayer is not convenient nor is it intended to be self-satisfying or self-serving. It is about the giving of one's attention, time, and heart to the one most worthy of carefully crafted words. Unfortunately, it is a lost "art." We share our burden, we draw attention to our concerns, we give our "two cents," and then we generally say "amen." Our prayers often intend to unleash our potential greatness rather than to proclaim His. They are defined by our concerns rather than His. They say much more about what we think about our situations than how we feel about Him. In this climate of self-centered (and sometimes self-indulgent) prayer, we should expect most of them to go unanswered. Yet somehow, we continue to be disappointed and often distance ourselves from this most precious of gifts. It is time for people to pray correctly, especially ministers!

To pray on His terms rather than our own and to make God—and not our desires—the main point of prayer must become priority number 1. First, we must look at how not to pray before we can begin to forge a path toward godly prayer. What will result is an understanding that prayer is something that is quite hard to master but is well worth the effort. People will begin to look forward to their time of prayer and hate to say, "Amen." This is how God intended divine human fellowship to be. In a world where mediocre prayer abounds, our goal must be to pray correctly and effectively. This is the type of prayer that God wants to listen to.

Biblical Case Studies on How Not to Pray

We have all heard well-meaning, God-fearing folks say that there is no wrong way to pray. The truth that is intended in this statement is that imperfect prayer is better than no prayer at all. I would not disagree in principle with this basic truth, but fear that it has greatly damaged the church, which now barely survives due in part to a consistent choice to take the path of least resistance regarding prayer. The unfortunate reality is that we live in a culture where mediocrity is the new level of acceptability. This cannot be tolerated in issues of faith and is entirely unacceptable in regard to prayer.

Prayers are unanswered for many different reasons. In some cases, God has a better view of the future and has chosen the best over the good. The apostle Paul gives us ample evidence of this reality in several instances. First, God would not allow Paul to go home to heaven because he was considered more useful on earth (Philippians 1:23–24). As well, we see Paul denied a thrice-repeated plea to have his "thorn" removed. Here we see that God does not mind so much if his children tend to walk with a bit of a limp and are rightly forced to recognize their greatness is His presence and not their abilities. In another instance, Paul desired to go to Rome and work among the Christians there freely and then move on to Spain, but ultimately came to Rome in chains, and many believe he never made it to Spain. Luke portrays that Paul was quite successful in his circumstances and was, once again, forced to be more effective in the long run by being limited for a short time. Clearly, some prayers remain unanswered for divine reasons.

However, the Bible also demonstrates another type of unanswered prayer. Not one that holds off small blessing for future greatness, but where an individual or group is denied heavenly assistance or even access for other, more dubious reasons. Some might assume that effective, eloquent prayer is standard issue for a believer. If a quick glance around American Evangelical's prayer lives does not destroy that theory, perhaps the reality that Jesus's disciples did not consider this common knowledge should succeed in changing our minds. In Luke 11:1–13, the disciples noticed how Jesus prays and are convinced that this is a skill that they have yet to develop. So they asked Him, "Lord, teach us to pray." The answer was the Lord's Prayer. If we hope to be effective at this spiritual discipline, we must ask to be taught as well. An effective prayer life is not "standard issue," nor is it a "natural talent." It is rather a labor of love.

Scripture is filled with details about prayer warriors as well as those whose prayers were rejected by God. A look at this group of ineffective worshippers is imperative to understanding how prayers can be rejected by God for various reasons.

Character Matters: King Saul

The story of King Saul is tragic. History has not been kind to Israel's first king and for good reason. Here are a few details about Saul that are essential to understanding his stunted prayer life. The following is by no means a comprehensive list but does demonstrate the differing levels of failure during his life.

1. He was a shepherd that could not find his own donkeys (1 Samuel 9:3–20).
2. He hid himself in the luggage on his inauguration day (1 Samuel 10:22).
3. He overstepped his position by offering a sacrifice before the Lord instead of waiting for Samuel to come (1 Sam 13:7–14).
4. He foolishly forbid his armies to eat and be strengthened and was willing to kill his own son, Jonathan, over the issue (1 Samuel 14:23–45).
5. Saul did not understand his limited role as king and showed poor judgment by keeping back some animals (for sacrifice) and accepted King Agog's surrender in a battle where he was instructed to kill everything (1 Samuel 15:1–35). This grieved God, who viewed this as an act of betrayal (15:11).
6. He showed limited bravery by allowing a young David to go out to meet Goliath (but did offer his armor, at least!) (1 Samuel 17:31–40).
7. Saul became obsessed with David and attempted to kill him several times, eventually abandoning his responsibility to protect Israel and chose to protect his position instead (1 Samuel 19–24). This became his sole obsession.
8. He turned on his own son, Jonathan, who rightly believed David to be the next king (1 Samuel 20:30–34).

9. He murdered priests because they gave David provisions (1 Samuel 22).
10. He had no discernment when choosing to speak to a witch about spiritual matters (1 Samuel 28:1–25). In this instance (as well as others), he showed that prayer was something that he only desired when he was in trouble and needed mercy.
11. He took matters into his own hand once again at his death, taking his own life after being wounded and knowing that defeat was imminent (1 Samuel 31:1–6).

Saul was a man who was higher in stature than the average Hebrew (1 Samuel 9:2), had less spiritual depth than an average Hebrew, had less knowledge of the Torah than an average Hebrew, and therefore possessed less moral clarity than an average Hebrew. Clearly, Israel was given what they had asked for, a "King like all the other nations have."

One incident in particular stands out when we look at God's rejection of Saul. God had already rejected him as King. After God rejects Saul as king for his consistent disobedience and sends Samuel to anoint David, Saul finds that he can no longer communicate with God. He asks Samuel to assist, but he refuses.

> "Now therefore, please pardon my sin and return with me, that I may worship the lord." But Samuel said to Saul, "I will not return with you; for you have rejected the word of the lord, and the lord has rejected you from being king over Israel" (1 Samuel 15:24–26).

God was finished with Saul. Saul had no more chances.

Although there is much to discuss in regard to Saul, the matter at hand is prayer. In his darkest hour, when he should be able to throw himself in desperation at the mercy of God, he is not speechless but rather clueless. His prayers for forgiveness and his desire to remain as king were tied together in this event. Samuel showed him mercy, but God had rejected him. Here are a few defining characteristics and attitudes that led to this unanswered prayer.

1. Saul loved himself more than he loved God.
2. Saul had an opportunity to follow God but chose instead to do things on his terms, even such important things as worship, sacrifice, and offering.
3. The king refused the will of God when he knew that David had been anointed the next king.
4. Saul was only a man of action when it included his plan, his desire, and his benefit.
5. Saul did not demonstrate or desire discernment of God's will.
6. Saul was a jealous, petty, and bitter person.
7. Saul held hatred in his heart.
8. When Saul decided to be religious, he was thoughtless and substanceless in his action.
9. Saul's prayer life was not about developing a relationship with God but rather beseeching the Lord for constant help when everything else had failed. Prayer, for Saul, was always a "last resort."

The summary of Saul's reign is a mixed bag. Israel won some and lost some. However, the sum of Saul as a man was a sad story in unmet potential that finds little, if any, redemption in the end. Granted, it is hard to succeed when you reign between God and David. However, the most clear summary of Saul's life and contribution is what is found, or rather not found, in 1 Chronicles 2 that begins with the genealogy of David, skipping any record of Saul's monarchy altogether. A life that cannot be reined in, one that is defined by personal preference and promotion, is a life that God cannot bless, will not enrich, and will refuse to make great by denying the privilege of healthy divine communication. Saul ended his life as it had been lived, on his terms, in his time—sad, empty, and eerily silent, void of God's input. A life without healthy prayer is a life void of God's presence.

Motivation Matters: Jonah

Like King Saul, Jonah is a mixed bag at best! Rarely do we read about a greater revival in the history of the world. At the same time, do we ever see God move so mightily in spite of His chosen prophet's disinterest? Jonah had great aspirations for his people. Along with this, he desired God to unleash his fury on their greatest enemy, Ninevah. However, God and Jonah were not on the same page. God did desire to send revival to one and an indictment to the other, but it was the direct opposite of Jonah's hope. Although we do not read an actual prayer of Jonah, it is clear by his response to God's call that he and God probably had discussed these matters before. Regardless, God was not interested in giving Jonah his wish. This is a common theme among the prophets, including Jeremiah, Isaiah, Daniel, Hosea, and others.

There was nothing unusual about Jonah's expectations. A simple reading of the Torah and earlier prophecies would most likely lead the prophet to his adopted view. Add this to David's imprecatory Psalms and you have the making of a prophet who was ready for judgment day—on someone else! One could understand his utter disappointment at God's shocking call. A few things should be pointed out concerning Jonah's unanswered prayer.

1. Jonah assumed his enemies were God's enemies and that God would deem them unlovable.
2. Jonah had not yet reached a point of spiritual maturity that would allow him to be obedient to a call that was against his convictions.
3. Jonah thought he could respond to an unanswered prayer by abandoning God's call.

4. Jonah preached halfheartedly, knowing (and fearing) that God would save his enemies.
5. Jonah displayed great selfishness throughout the process and even until the end.
6. Jonah's hand was forced, and a true prayer of repentance came from his heart. He was not over his disappointment, however.

God cannot answer a prayer that is against His character nor one that is against His revealed will. Jonah did not have to ask for God's will to be shown, it was abundantly clear.

In the end, motivation does matter for right prayer. We must be motivated by what motivates God, compassion, forgiveness, and second chances. We should be quite careful about wishing people gone, welcoming "blessed subtractions," and deeming folks "enemies of God" because we see them as our enemies. Redemption is always a good goal and a great topic of prayer. God loves to talk about redemption of evil people, perhaps we should join Him!

Content Matters: Job

Job is known for his patience unless you carefully read his story! He is rightly noted for his endurance, but patience in the manner that we understand it was not one of his finer qualities. If it is true that Job handled his situation well, then explaining God's angry answer out of the whirlwind and the storm is impossible. However, if Job's requests were suspect in nature, then God's rebuke followed by His blessing becomes a more consistent scenario. Clearly, Job had some things right and some things wrong. A look at both is imperative. Job was right in the following responses:

1. He did not blame God or curse God.
2. He accepted God's will.
3. He remained righteous.

4. He asked for a clearer understanding of God.
5. He sought truth at all costs.
6. He rebuked the retribution theology of his friends.
7. He wanted to see God and work things out.

However, Job did behave in some ways that were improper. He spoke to God (prayed) mostly through his conversation with his "friends" that revealed that Job still had some growing to do and indeed had much yet to learn.

1. He cursed the day that he was born.
2. He claimed to be deserving of better.
3. He went overboard in defending himself against his friends' wrong accusations.
4. He continued to live in the past.
5. He gave God an ultimatum, "vindicate me or kill me."
6. He threw himself a pity party.

It is clear by God's response toward Job that He was unhappy with Job and planned on putting him in his place. He did not show up giving Job answers, but rather asking him questions. He did not show up with reassurance of His love, but rather wrath that stemmed from His holiness. Note the tone and content of what He says.

Perhaps we are getting a response from our Father in heaven, but we don't recognize that He is responding to our complaints with some questions of His own. Who do we think we are? Why are we blaming Him? Do we really know as much about the situation as we think we do? What is our goal in life, to succeed or to see Him? These are all fair questions to ask of one who believes himself to be righteous. Perhaps listening to God's response, His conviction, and His disappointment in us may go much farther than just sharing our many questions of justice with Him.

Many more examples of unanswered prayer are found throughout Scripture including the Pharisees, Sadducees, and Scribes. We learn through them and Jesus's rebuke of them that other things matter for a healthy prayer life as well: sincerity, humility, theology, justice, brokenness, and more. God is not required to listen to prayers from just anyone. We are in the throne room of the King of all Kings and the attitude, presentation, and substance of what we say matters greatly.

What Prayer Isn't: Our Misconceptions about Prayer

Prayer is something we are all quite familiar with as a phenomenon but not as a concept. Wading through the muck of presupposition and assumption is not going to be easy, but it should be viewed as mandatory and will prove quite helpful. To complete this journey, a handful of realities must be faced.

1. We falsely assume that prayer is a simple proposition and can be carried out with ease.
2. Prayers too often have no substance because they do not follow the biblical models.
3. Many prayers have become too human focused and far too many prayers, especially corporate ones, are an exercise in self-communication rather than divine communication. We must stop talking to and about ourselves and give Him more focus.
4. Many prayers are being prayed without proper credentials. We come in the name of Christ and through the blood of Christ. Our prayers must be focused primarily on Him and the privilege we are allowed through His sacrifice.
5. Many are being lifted up with wrong motives.

6. Far too many prayers are not on topic. We are not talking about what is on God's heart and mind.

7. When Christians do pray on topic, they often focus on minor issues rather than the major ones.

8. Prayers are all too often spoken in one of two extremes; memorized liturgy or "freestyle." A good balance between the two must be reached.

Indeed, prayer is not natural to our humanity. There is nothing natural about the way the Bible commands us to pray, and there is very little spiritual about the way we've been taught and currently practice prayer. These words might seem accusatory and abrasive, but the prayer life of our nation is on life support due to our lack of understanding and years of accepting the reality that only certain people are called to be prayer warriors and the rest of us can call them when we really need divine intervention. In the world that daily stares us in the face, we are far beyond such simple sentiments.

Few periods in history have needed prayer more than we do right now in postmodern America. Few ministers have been as desperate for effective prayer as we are now. One need not have any doubt that God is willing to come into our confined, small, and relatively insignificant world, speak our language, and walk with us. He did this through the incarnate Christ and continues the journey through His Holy Spirit. Even so, our approach to prayer begs a serious question that will determine our approach to our faith as a whole, "Did God come into our world so we could bring Him to our level or did He enter our world as a Savior to bring us into His?" Clearly, God came to our level, but it was a rescue mission to break us free from our prison. He did not come to reside behind our prison walls indefinitely; He came instead to "bust us out." Prayer is an ever-present reminder that we are free indeed. Unfortunately, our prayers are voiced like we are still in jail.

What We Learn from Paul About Prayer

Now that we've seen the wrong way to pray, it is useful to think of the right methods and attitudes to carry with us toward the throne of grace. If we can show the opposite attitudes of Saul, Jonah, and Job, if we can be humble, patient, and broken, then we will have a hearing. Jesus guarantees this for us.

Our attitude of boldness comes from Him, but it is He who at the same time makes us humble. If we come with the right attitude, we have a good start, but it is only a start. The rest is about methodology and substance. Three Pauline prayers will define what healthy prayer should look like and will thus pave the path that we must journey toward profound prayer. Consider the following examples:

> For this reason I too, having heard of the faith in the Lord Jesus which exists among you and your love for all the saints, do not cease giving thanks for you, while making mention of you in my prayers; that the God of our Lord Jesus Christ, the Father of glory, may give to you a spirit of wisdom and of revelation in the knowledge of Him. I pray that the eyes of your heart may be enlightened, so that you will know what is the hope of His calling, what are the riches of the glory of His inheritance in the saints, and what is the surpassing greatness of His power toward us who believe. These are in accordance with the working of the strength of His might which He brought about in Christ, when He raised Him from the dead and seated Him at His right hand in the heavenly places, far above all rule and authority and power and dominion, and every name that is named, not only in this age but also in the one to come. And He put all things in subjection under His feet, and gave Him as head over all things to the church, which is His body, the fullness of Him who fills all in all. (Ephesians 1:15–23)

Although it has been established that Paul held a special place in his heart for the Ephesians, he prayed just as passionately and personally for other churches as well. Note his prayer on behalf of the Philippians.

> I thank my God in all my remembrance of you, always offering prayer with joy in my every prayer for you all, For I am confident of this very thing, that He who began a good work in you will perfect it until the day of Christ Jesus. And this I pray, that your love may abound still more and more in real knowledge and all discernment, so that you may approve the things that are excellent, in order to be sincere and blameless until the day of Christ; having been filled with the fruit of righteousness which comes through Jesus Christ, to the glory and praise of God. (Philippians 1:3, 5, 7–11)

As well, many common themes are confirmed and solidified in his brief prayer for the Colossian church.

> We give thanks to God, the Father of our Lord Jesus Christ, praying always for you…For this reason also, since the day we heard of it, we have not ceased to pray for you and to ask that you may be filled with the knowledge of His will in all spiritual wisdom and understanding, so that you will walk in a manner worthy of the Lord, to please Him in all respects, bearing fruit in every good work and increasing in the knowledge of God; strengthened with all power, according to His glorious might, for the attaining of all steadfastness and patience; joyously giving thanks to the Father, who has qualified us to share in the inheritance of the saints in Light. (Colossians 1:3, 9–12)

Paul shows great consistency in every aspect of his faith, including prayer. Note the common themes of these apostolic prayers.

1. Thanksgiving for believers is key.
2. He prays for the greatest need of believers, wisdom, and spiritual insight. He does not place health as a priority, but focuses instead on a prayer for their greatest need, to

receive grace enough to know and understand God despite our humanity.

3. The goal of his prayer is clear. He wants believers to be ready to meet Christ and while they wait for that glorious moment, to serve Him effectively.

4. His prayer is utterly and completely Christocentric. This is evident leading into each prayer and going away from each prayer. Christ was Paul's life. This is what all believers need more than anything. We have Christ. We just need the insight to desire, know, and submit to Him completely.

It is amazing that great prayers offered by ministers as intercession for their parishioners can be summarized under four major themes! Think for a moment about the way we pray for other believers. Do our prayers hold these Pauline priorities? It seems that Paul's prayers were grounded in a dual depth of love of Christ and of His bride. No minister was more accused, betrayed, and hurt by the church than Paul. Paul indeed rebuked when needed, but his love for people was seen throughout his ministry, specifically through the substance of his prayers.

As ones who are called to intercede on behalf of God's people, even during our darkest times in our own personal lives, ministers stand in desperate need of education and training regarding prayer. Our prayers need to move from self-centered to God-centered and other-centered. This will grow us closer together, give us endurance in our struggles, and ultimately pull our congregation together. A look at Paul's prayers for the Philippians, Colossians, and Ephesians demonstrates how both priorities can be achieved at the same time. These prayers demonstrate requests that are on the mind and heart of God and remind humans that we have far to go in becoming effective prayer warriors.

Prayer for postmodern evangelicals has very little in common with the prayers of the New Testament. It is time to evaluate what we're doing. We pray mainly intercessory prayers about health or safety issues. There is nothing wrong with praying for the sick. However, no one seems to be getting healed! Ironically enough, we seem to be all right with that and just keep on praying in a way that is not moving God to answer. Most logical minds should question why God does not answer our prayers. Consider the following two telling realities. First, believers today tend to approach prayer as a fait accompli and submit to God's will before we even ask Him for anything. Submission is primary, but we are called to make our requests known to God and to pray without doubt. Second, we have stopped praying for healing and begun praying for peace and comfort. In our prayers, we've given up on God's divine intervention. Since our prayers are primarily intercession for the sick and have been for some time, one would think that we are getting extremely good results. This could not be farther from the truth.

11

Be Spirit-led in Your Ministry

I do not mean to appoint myself as a critic of ministers, ministries, and churches. In fact, I'm a big fan of all three! However, even as I believe and predict great things for the American church in the future, I cannot seem to shake the feeling that something very important is missing. In many churches, we have a foundation of orthodoxy and biblical inerrancy, we focus on evangelism, we preach the word, minister to the downcast, etc., etc. However, even in the most obedient of churches, things still don't look quite right. It seems a bit odd, but what is being omitted is our greatest need—a comprehensively biblical theology of the Holy Spirit and openness to His leading. For the most part, we do not know how to be "spiritual" because we are not quite sure what this means. This would perhaps explain why ministry has become so difficult for both pastor and parishioner. We are in need of a pneumatology lesson in the most serious way.[47] Unless we understand the foundation and work of the Spirit, we can forget about our churches ever being healthy.

The Biblical Call to Spirituality

Current understanding of the Spirit is often defined by extremes. There is a tendency among some to depersonalize the Spirit where he often becomes referred to as "it," an impersonal force or expression of God rather than His very Spirit. For these people, the Spirit is a distant reality, not an immanent one. For others, it is a habit of overemphasizing His gifts and mysterious role within Christianity above His person as described in Scripture. With this view, many other things in the life of the believer and life of the church are ignored so that the pursuit of the Spirit can be given full attention. However, it seems that few find the biblical balance that defines spirituality for us and our ministries.

True spirituality and the Christian life should be understood as synonymous terms. The Spirit's role was defined clearly by Jesus in John's Gospel, chapters 14–16. He spoke of the role of the Spirit—to convict of sin, righteousness, and judgment. Christ also gave detail concerning His duty—to empower, comfort, and lead. However, the ultimate reality of the Spirit's purpose is that He will testify of Christ to human beings. Jesus stated that his exit and the Spirit's entrance would benefit believers. With all that the Spirit brings, including power, conviction, insight, discernment, etc., the most important work of the Spirit is the revelation to people of Christ. Simply put, to be spiritual is to know Christ in the manner that the Bible, and thus God, expects. It leads to a life that is lived beyond the flesh—superseding the world—and always aware of and sensitive to the leading of God's Spirit. It is *anything* but the quintessential Christian life as it is defined, taught, and patterned today.

Since the Spirit is the most personal member of the Trinity, the apostle Paul makes the various churches of his day aware of some very specific expectations and clarifies some serious misconceptions. Even though He is mysterious and difficult to grasp on many levels for the Christian, the apostle unapologetically tells the Ephesians to "Pray in the Spirit" (Ephesians 6:18). As well, the Philippians are commanded to "worship in the Spirit" (Philippians 3:3). He also gives the far-reaching call to the Galatians to "walk in the Spirit" (Galatians 5:16). Paul expects the Christian's life to be one lived "in the Spirit." The absence of these realities can and will lead to great struggle, especially for the minister.

We must both realize and emphasize that these promises of the spiritual life also come with some instruction. Paul exhorts that one should be "filled with the Spirit" (Ephesians 5:18). By using the present active participle, Paul encourages this to be an action that is continual in nature and not just a one-time experience such as baptism in the Spirit. The failure to be filled with God's Spirit is to reject true knowledge of Christ and a genuine relationship with the Father. Ministers must be spiritual in every aspect of their life, or they will cease to be useful to the Kingdom of God. To not be spiritual is, in all reality, not to be genuinely Christian. It is not simply the Spirit's job to reveal Christ as Messiah, but also to reveal Him as purifier, refiner, friend, and ultimately, as judge of the world. To miss this is to miss the essence of Christ. Therefore, sinning against the Spirit is quite serious and highly dangerous as well.

Scripture reveals that there are many different sins that can be committed against the Holy Spirit. It is possible to lie to the Holy Spirit, as Ananias and Sapphira did (Acts 5:3–4). Paul speaks of the sins of grieving the Spirit (Ephesians 4:30) and quenching the Spirit (1 Thessalonians 5:19). Stephen accuses his adversaries of always resisting the Holy Spirit (Acts 7:51). Each offense has a different substance, description, and serious consequence.

1. *Grieving the Holy Spirit.* Even before Pentecost, the act of rebellion has grieved God's Spirit. The consequence of this behavior was God's wrath found usually in the punishment of his rebellious people. The most often quoted instance is found in Isaiah 63:10, "But they rebelled and grieved His Holy Spirit; therefore He turned Himself to become their enemy and fought against them." Ultimately, the grief of God's Spirit brought about the wrath and anger

of God upon His own Son on the cross, allowing salvation for God's elect. After the Spirit's descent on Pentecost, the crime of grieving was to be understood as even more serious than ever.

Paul commanded the Ephesians to be unified, church living, with a holy purpose for God. Toward the end of the letter, within a litany of exhortations in the heart of the Epistle, Paul gives the simple command, "Do not grieve the Holy Spirit by whom you have been sealed for the day of redemption" (Ephesians 4:30). The grieving of the Holy Spirit is indeed a relational event. For the believer, the connection with the Spirit is intimate and so too is the reaction when it is not attended to in a proper manner. As ministers, the sin has even further-reaching consequences. It is noteworthy that the apostle does not warn the Ephesians not to anger or frustrate the Spirit, but rather asked them to avoid grieving Him instead. Grief is personal. It is a mixed emotion and can be quite complex, but everybody knows how it feels.

Since the command is surrounded by many specific exhortations, some before (concerning anger, concerning stealing, concerning greed, and concerning proper speech) and some following (bitterness, rage, anger, brawling, slander, and malice), we can logically conclude from this that the Spirit is grieved by a believer's yielding to sin. Therefore, grieving of the Spirit is most importantly a supernatural result caused by fleshly indulgences. Paul had made it clear to the Ephesians that Satan was a real enemy and spirituality a real calling. When we fail, it does not just affect us, but Him as well.

2. *Quenching the Holy Spirit.* Like Ephesus, Thessalonica was a difficult place to minister. Also, like the Ephesian call to not grieve the Holy Spirit, the Thessalonian call to avoid quenching the Spirit comes both at the end of the letter and in the midst of a list of exhortations. The warning is most

likely referring to sin in general. The subject at hand is indeed grave. It was created by a behavior among those within the church that choked and virtually extinguished the work of the Spirit by their resistance to Him.[48] It should not be seen as only a laity issue, but we must recognize it as a pastoral transgression as well. The absence of the Spirit's unhindered work would cause the church-manifold problems, and Paul's tone demonstrates this both here and elsewhere.

The original language of 1 Thessalonians 5:19 regarding a warning of "quenching" the Spirit can carry different meanings and some disagreement does exist. The best option is to apply it in reference to the common description of the Spirit as fire (Matthew 3:11, Luke 3:16, Acts 2:3), allowing it to carry the idea of not "extinguishing" the Spirit's potent and effective power. Current application offered for "quenching" includes a wide array of utilization: stifling, repressing, holding back, squelching, choking, and muffling. The point is rather clear, wrong behavior can interfere with the Spirit's work within the church.

Although the two have some differences, it is important to note that quenching the Spirit and grieving the spirit are connected on some level.

> Quenching is what you do to the Spirit, grieving is how He responds to what you did...You do not quench the Holy Spirit without grieving the Holy Spirit and you will not grieve the Holy Spirit unless you quench the Holy Spirit... one describes what you do, the other describes what He does. You quench, He grieves...He grieves because you quench.[49]

When God decided to express Himself in a way that would enhance both His Old and New Covenant revelation, he chose the Holy Spirit, a piece of Himself. It is clear that rebuffing such a personal gesture by either hindering or resisting Him would clearly bring grief to

Him. It is sad that we spend so much time reflecting on our own heartache and very little on His.

Living in the Spirit

Ministers must look to be not only leaders, but models when it comes to the Spirit-filled life. If the Holy Spirit is going to find His proper place in our ministry and church, it must begin with our lives. We must move beyond the centuries-old discussion that centers only on the "charismatic" gifts spoken of within the New Testament Epistles. It is a debate that has caused much strife and separation. However, we've talked, preached, and debated it to death. Perhaps it is time to look deeper into the doctrine of the Spirit's role and seek definitions regarding the foundational issues of the Spirit's work among the individual believer as well as the church at large, both in individual morality and in the illumination of God's Word. Perhaps a few words in this direction can move us away from our historically fruitless discussions.

1. *The Role of the Holy Spirit.* A basic theology of the Spirit's role in the life and work of the minister must start when Christ introduced Him and His work. Jesus clearly stated that the believer would benefit from the departure of the Christ and the entrance of the *Paraclete* (John 14:26). In his final discourse, He explained why this would be so. First and foremost, Jesus shared that the Spirit would continue to testify of Christ, His teaching, and His work (John 15:26) and would guide believers into all truth (John 16:13). The most important work of the Spirit was, and is, His revelatory work concerning the mystery of the Gospel and the disclosure of Jesus as not only the Jewish Messiah but also the Savior of the world.

    The secondary work of the Spirit in the life of the believer is sanctification. The Holy Spirit is the point at which the Trinity becomes personal in the life of the believer. It is the

Spirit's guidance, comfort, empowering, and equipping of the saints that allows them to live up to the expectations of their Creator. Jesus explains what the Spirit's role would be. And He, when He comes, will convict the world concerning sin and righteousness and judgment: concerning sin because they do not believe in Me; concerning righteousness because I go to the Father and you no longer see Me; and concerning judgment because the ruler of this world had been judged. (John 16:8–11). The Spirit works to save us and make us holy.

We begin our relationship with the Spirit when He introduces us to Christ, however, it must not end there. Unfortunately, I do believe that many Christians have left the Spirit behind with a false understanding that He is now "tame" since we know Christ. Nothing could be farther from the truth. The absence of the Spirit's work in the life of the church is the reason that so many churches are dying and so many people of the faith are disinterested. A renewal is needed in a most desperate way.

2. *The Fruit of the Spirit.* Among the other biblical writers, Paul elaborates on this role of the Spirit within human morality more than anyone. Among the chief of the passages that reveal this, Galatians 5:25 is the most succinct and powerful, "If we live by the Spirit, let us also walk by the Spirit." A similar call to "walk in the Spirit" was also given prior to the discussion in 5:16. It is there that the plain truth is offered, if one walks by the Spirit, the deeds of the flesh will not be carried out. Paul's concern is primarily ethical regarding this church that had been infiltrated by Judaizers seeking to legalize the faith. He demands that the believers seek out a spiritual ethic, not a carnal one. Paul wants to demonstrate clearly that it is the Holy Spirit who provides the godly life required in the law.

Galatians 5 teaches us a rather simple truth, the Holy Spirit is the all-encompassing gift from God and He is the foundation for all of the virtue in the believer's life. Christ is our Savior, the Spirit is God's presence within us and our daily guide. The fruits themselves serve as our "ground rules" to proper Christian attitudes and behavior. The reality is that love, joy, peace, patience, kindness, goodness, faithfulness, gentleness, and self-control are found interwoven into the life of every believer. Without the Spirit behind the list of virtuous fruit, it is simply reduced to a list of moral ideals that are clearly unachievable. Indeed, these are virtues sought by many religions, in many different ways. The fruit of the Spirit challenges individuals to become the kind of believer who will "follow the rules" without thought. This is so desperately needed in our churches today.

3. *The Gifts of the Spirit.* We've focused far too long on the Gifts of the Spirit in an unhealthy manner. There are some twenty *charismata* or spiritual gifts mentioned in four passages of the New Testament: 1 Corinthians 12:8–10 and 28–30; Romans 12:6–8; Ephesians 4:11; and 1 Peter 4:11. We spend our time talking about only one or two, the controversial ones. We need to revisit the question, why do we need gifts from God and why did He give them to us?

- They are intended to empower the individual to bring more glory to God through their discipleship.
- Spiritual gifts reveal that certain people have special abilities that are intended to serve God that others do not. This reveals that God is sovereign in all that he does, even in the dispensing of talents and gifts, as well as defining roles among His children. The irony of the differences within the body is that each part is needed, each role must be filled, and each person must understand their part if success is to be eternal.
- Finally, and perhaps most importantly, the diverse gifts of the Holy Spirit are intended to shape and strengthen

a community and thus are central to communal unity and morality.
- They build up the body.

While it is true that Jesus and his moral teaching are clearly at the heart of the New Testament, the emphasis in the Bible seems more concerned with how it can be possible for ordinary men and women who have passed from death to life to live the life of Christ in an alien and antagonistic world. The solution to the charge that the ethics of Jesus are impossible for people is quite simply the person and work of the Holy Spirit. He is the source of the power and capacity to be like Jesus. Without the Spirit, this new life is not a reality. We as ministers cannot forget this. If we capture the essence of this divine reality, our ministries can take flight in ways that we never dreamed.

12

Let the Profound Define You

The word *profound* has always grabbed me. I guess it is one of those interests that we all have that we can't quite explain. Ever since I was young, I wanted to be profound, I sought the profound, and I demanded the profound from others. My frustration was that I grew up in Middle America in the "Bible belt" where our existence is often described as the "simple life." I've never been accused of being over-intellectual. However, I've always wanted to be challenged. If I am going to read a book, I want it to say something new. If I am going to hear a sermon or lecture, I want it to take things to another level. If I am going to have a conversation with someone, I want depth. The profound for me has always been a deep well that I could drink from anytime, and I knew where to find it again when my thirst came back. A small number of certain people, authors, and preachers have always challenged my intellect, and I am eternally grateful to them. However, postmodern Evangelicals have not been profound about much for quite a long time.[50] Although, as both professor and preacher, I believe that we are getting better.

The word *profound* has many meanings. It comes from two separate words in Latin that mean "before" and "bottom." The idea is that we are getting to the bottom of things and the profound is the way to get there. *Merriam-Webster* defines profound in the following ways: "having intellectual depth, difficult to comprehend, having a feeling of intensity or quality."[51] Intellectual depth should be right up our alley as Christian ministers. We can get to the bottom of things with the most insightful resources available exclusively to us including the Bible, the Holy Spirit, and the salvation history of the church. Unfortunately, we have far too often chosen to stay only on the surface so that everyone could understand what is being said. I do believe it is essential that we present the Gospel in an understandable way. Nonetheless, in the process of surface teaching, preaching, and church life, we've lost millions. Some have shunned us, others have left us, and still others still come to church but "checked out" long ago.

Profound, expository preaching, and teaching are essential in challenging the intellect. Don't get me wrong, both evangelistic and practical living preaching is great, but only for winning converts or giving the milk of the Word to babes and not for making disciples. Evangelism and discipleship are both distinct elements of the Great Commission. Perhaps a new approach can broaden our net and more can be gathered into the boat in the future, and while they are there, we can actually show them how to fish the deep waters themselves.

The Problem with Spiritual Simplicity

We often live by the adage, "The simpler the better!" In theory, this sentiment sounds fine. Nonetheless, there is a world of difference between trying to make Christianity uncomplicated and making it simple. Uncomplicated things can still be quite profound. However, simple things will always be simple. I fear we've done the latter with our faith.

Clearly, God has given access for everyone to the Gospel. That does not mean He has made its content easy to digest. Apparently, Jesus's own disciples were often confused for a good part of the three years that they spent together. They understood many of the basics, but other aspects were quite confusing, and Christ didn't always get down on their level to give them a quick lesson. Recall Jesus's final discourse in John 14–16 and note this dialogue toward the end.

> "These things I have spoken to you in figurative language; an hour is coming when I will no longer speak to you in figurative language, but will tell you plainly of the Father...I came forth from the Father and have come into the world; I am leaving the world again and going to the Father." His disciples said, "Lo, now You are speaking plainly and are not using a figure of speech. Now we know that You know all things, and have no need for anyone to question You; by this we believe that You came from God." Jesus answered them, "Do you now believe?" (John 16:25–31)

The disciples obviously did not think that Jesus was making things easy on them! With this in mind, we too must not confuse access and comprehension. An individual's understanding of the faith is to come through the Holy Spirit and not just our attempts to explain doctrine.

Anytime Christians have tried to oversimplify the complex nature of the Gospel, it has had disastrous consequences. When we place human access of truth ahead of the actual theological truth of Scripture, we cast pearls before swine. If you think of past attempts to make the Gospel less complicated, it is clear that these attempts have resulted in only more complication. We start with good intentions and we end with liberalism, overemotional experientialism, fundamentalism, and legalism. Carl F. H. Henry rightly stated regarding the "Jesus Freaks" of the seventies, "Their shallow doctrinal logic left them vulnerable. Their plea for an uncomplicated Christianity involved more complications than they could see."[52]

Why Must We Be Profound?

The pendulum in the church has swung away from the profound and toward the simple for several generations now. In part, this is due to the fact that Christianity in America has been reduced to the religion of the "simple life" and "simple folk." However, we as leaders have sometimes confused simple with stupid. We preach to the lowest common denominator and wonder why our people are not growing! Either our people are obstinate or they are ignorant. We've far too long used the former as a cop-out for the latter. We are responsible for being profound to a level that gives them a passion for the things of God. It is our job to make them hungry for the Word! Our people do not need theology explained to them on a third grade level. They need the meat of the Word to survive on as adults. Consider the following rationale for seeking a profound ministry.

1. *Our God is not simple.* A look a creation, even a glance at Scripture and a quick study of the human body will clue us in to the reality of an intelligent Creator that never misses a detail and insists on challenging our intellect every moment of each day. God is *extremely* profound. His is sovereignly omniscient. And He calls us to *know* Him. Not to know about Him, but to truly know Him. In this knowledge, we should reach a depth of understanding that cannot be described any other way than, "having intellectual depth, difficult to comprehend, having a feeling of intensity or quality."

2. *God did not create us to be simple either.* We were created in His image to be like Him! All humans are defined in part by their intelligence. Some do not live up to their mental capacity, but our species is separated by all others in regard to our level of intellectual abilities. We have been given the capacity to know God, understand His calling, and follow in His way. Those who have been adopted by God must be

profound. These are family rules. As we are sanctified, we should grow deeper in our thinking and in our methods. As we become like Him, we should become incomprehensible and inexplicable in our faith, in our ability to love, and in our insistence on serving and forgiving one another.

3. *We are called to love God with all of our minds.* We have different levels of maturity in love including heart, soul, mind, and strength. I've always thought of those healed by Christ, jumping up and down, vibrant and excited, as those with "heart love." They were emotionally tied to Christ! He was their king, and nothing would ever happen that could separate them. Their hearts beat for Him alone. Unfortunately, sometimes these seeds sprout and do not take root. But, heart love is the first step.

King David's many Psalms of "soul longing" demonstrate what "soul love" looks like. It is beyond mere emotion. The entire being of the person is involved in longing for God. We cannot get enough of Him. The spiritual "infatuation" of heart love has worn off years ago, and we are more in love than ever. We look to Him as our protection, our sustenance, our water, and our air.

Strength love is difficult, and I believe few Christians reach its full potential. Many are not even interested. I see Christ's Gethsemane prayer as strength love. When our body is laid bare before God and all that we are is His alone, then our lives are nothing. Paul wanted the sufferings because they gave Him something in common with Christ (Philippians 3:10). Then, and *only* then, can we say that "to live is Christ and to die is gain" (Philippians 1:21) from prison! This remains our goal and few Christians have attained it.

It is clear that we know many people with hearts like David, but few with the strength of Christ or Paul in his/her most desperate hour. Most Christians have either stopped at heart or soul or have never been challenged to go beyond our commitment level and our depth of desire. To be like Jesus in this respect, we must first love God with our mind. When I think of "mind love," I think of none other than the apostle Paul. Sit for a moment and recollect all the times that Paul used logic with his people. He logically refuted the legalism of the Judaizers in Galatia, the foolish dietary requirements in Rome, and the immoral living in Corinth. Think about how many times he asked, "Know ye not?" Remember how often he personally stated, "I have considered" or "I know" or "I have been persuaded…" The most profound passages in Romans (chapters 8 and 12) are filled with the result of his logic. He didn't *feel* that God would never forsake him; rather, he was *convinced* of it. He didn't just *think* it a good idea that we offer our bodies as living sacrifices, he thought that it was "reasonable worship." Paul's logic must come out when we preach from his texts. Our logic must be evident in how we teach, preach, counsel, pray, and minister. We must love the Lord with *all* of our minds, and this will spur in us the compulsion to think ourselves deeply toward the profound.

4. *Many true thinkers have turned away from the faith.* Since we have wrongly portrayed Christianity as a religion of emotion and simplicity, we have lost many people of logic and depth in the wake. We try to combat them with apologetics and political movements, but we seem unable to break through their barriers. Had I not grown up in one, I'm quite sure that most churches would not appeal to me. Many people have agreed. However, we have tried to be attractive by changing only our music, making our sermons less profound and more practical, and have removed parts of our sacrificial worship (offering) from the service altogether. We can choose to give them what we think they want, or we can offer them what

God offered us, the most intense reality known to man. We must take them to the "bottom" of the Gospel!

How Can We Be Profound?

Hopefully we are feeling a bit more urgency about being defined by a thoughtful journey toward the bottom of the Gospel! The question remains, "How do we get there?" I have a few ideas that might assist in moving toward the profound.

First, we can ask the question of "why" much more than we do. Traditionally, we have given the answer to this question with a simple response of, "Because." Although that may work for some children (it doesn't work with mine!), it is the wrong answer for people who God is drawing unto Himself. When we ask why, many doors appear before us. We can question why God said or did this at this particular time in history, was it said anywhere else, and how would He say it today. There is no doubt that most of us have just skimmed the surface of the Bible, we must go deeper. The very nature of Scripture and its author demand this.

A second path toward the insightful is to stop speaking to your people as if they cannot possibly comprehend what you are saying unless you illustrate everything for them. Although this is commonplace, it is perceived as both an insult and a waste of time to those who already get it or picked up on it the first time. Perhaps we should stop reaching toward the lowest common denominator in our preaching and illustration and instead bring everyone to a higher level of comprehension. The obvious cannot be profound unless presented in a new and fresh way. Everything does not need to be explained; assume they remember what you've previously said and only refer to it, don't belabor it.

Third, begin to interpret the Bible with itself by giving greater emphasis to the Old Testament in your preaching and teaching ministries. God has explained things well enough in His Word that it should be logically comprehensible by the reader. Remember, it is the Spirit who illumines the sermon, not the preacher. Use each testament to illustrate the other. Apply historical events from the OT to the New as Paul did regarding the character, nature, and work of God. As well, use the law to reiterate His expectation, the poetry section to remind them of how a true understanding of God leads to authentic worship, and employ the prophets to assure them that God knows what He's talking about and never forgets the details! The Old Testament is two-thirds of the Bible, it is rich and insightful. By preaching and teaching it, we are "getting to the bottom of things."

A fourth step would be to not make the application/invitation of the sermon or lesson so obvious by spelling it out. The application of a sermon is essential. However, it does not have to be narrow, specific, and/or elementary. We should apply the larger concepts of the sermon, ideas, concepts, and eternal truths and let the Holy Spirit make specific charges out of that in the heart and life of each of the hearers. After all, that is His job and not ours. When we give "three ways to respond to a sermon," we have limited what the Spirit can do, and we have done all of their work for them. When we say instead, "What do we learn about God or ourselves from this text?" we have made them think, and God will definitely attempt to demonstrate profound things to them.

A fifth path to "the bottom of things" is the most profound of all—*agape*. Although we've already discussed love in this book, it bears repeating that love is interwoven in to all that God has done and has consistently been involved in His dealings with us. If we will seek to move from a shallow to a deeper understanding of love, we will see how difficult it is to understand. However, a true understanding will make us more useful to the Kingdom. Love *never* fails! Once we begin to gain a greater understanding of love, we see both the intellectual and practical applied by God. It is a great place to start when taking our congregations on a journey to the bottom of theology.

The sixth focus that a minister should give to move toward the intellectually challenging is to be a powerful prayer warrior. We must utilize all types of prayer, not just intercession. We need to lead by personal example in confession, meditation, and in discerning God's leading. We should have a prayer life that allows us to have a basic sense of where God is leading the church. It must be an ongoing discussion. Let your conversation build on what God teaches you through Scripture, through study, through others, and through the nudging of the Holy Spirit. God moves in profound ways. Let Him lead you, and you'll begin to move toward the profound as well.

Finally, you should study! Find a theological topic or two that interests you and pursue them! What is your passion? Make it the congregation's passion as well. Don't pick some strange theological debate that has not been resolved for centuries. Rather, pick a character in the Bible, a book of the Bible, an attribute of God, or a common theme of God throughout Scripture and study it expositionally and deliver expository sermons. You will see a hunger for the Word become a common theme from the pews. Let the sermon preach to you first and then share with them what God has shown to you. Take your people in to your private study and personal research. They will trust you more, become more excited about what you are saying, and will draw closer to our King.

What we see in the above ideas is a constant theme throughout (I'm trying to be profound and insightful!). The theme is trust. We should trust our people and trust our God that they will do their specific jobs and fulfill the responsibilities that they have agreed to. If they know that we have faith in God and we trust them to live up to their commitments, perhaps they will. For too long the American pulpit has been highlighted with humor, illustration, and specific application. Again, there is nothing wrong with these tools in and of themselves. However, if we truly believe that the Spirit reveals and the Word does not return void, we should give them the spotlight.

The Ultimate Profoundness of Unity

We stand at a final impasse at this very moment. What hangs in the balance is the same issue that has been at a critical state since the ascension of Christ. Although our books, sermons, and discussions may give witness otherwise—the urgency is beyond our nation's identity, the threat of liberalism, or the decay of moral society. These are surface issues with deeper problems. What lies beneath our inner crumbling is at the heart of historic Christianity and relates to the very identity of the church herself. The bride of our Lord is losing herself in these times and has grown quite sick. This is due in great part to one major failing, we are no longer a community or a body, but rather a bunch of individuals just trying to get along.

What is God's greatest concern for the church? Imagine that we had surveillance in Heaven, what would the Trinity be talking about? What would the divine concern be for Christ's church? The path to understanding what God is thinking about now is to ask what He was thinking about the last time He revealed this to us. Recall the high priestly prayer of John 17. There He prayed for unity for us then as the key toward furthering the Gospel. It should be obvious to us that our unity is his greatest concern now and will continue to be until He returns.

All of our callings as believers are wrapped up in the community. It is the church that has the authority to storm the gates of hell, to fulfill the Great Commission, to remove those who would cause trouble within the fellowship, take care of the poor, act as stewards of the mysteries of God, and minister to her own needs. We have, for some reason, chosen to focus on self just as society does. Now we only proclaim that Jesus is *our personal* Lord and Savior rather than the Savior of the world or the husband of the church. We have fed ourselves with His love and cannot seem to love each other as a result. If we are to be effective and considered healthy in Heaven's eyes, we must be unified. Consider the following Scriptures on unity and compare our collective church experiences to Scripture's standard.

1 Corinthians 1:10: "Now I exhort you, brethren, by the name of our Lord Jesus Christ, that you all agree and that there be no divisions among you, but that you be made complete in the same mind and in the same judgment."

Ephesians 4:1–6: "Therefore I, the prisoner of the Lord, implore you to walk in a manner worthy of the calling with which you have been called, with all humility and gentleness, with patience, showing tolerance for one another in love, being diligent to preserve the unity of the Spirit in the bond of peace. There is one body and one Spirit, just as also you were called in one hope of your calling; one Lord, one faith, one baptism, one God and Father of all who is over all and through all and in all."

Ephesians 4:11–13: "It was he who gave some to be apostles, some to be prophets, some to be evangelists, and some to be pastors and teachers, to prepare God's people for works of service, so that the body of Christ may be built up until we all reach unity in the faith and in the knowledge of the Son of God and become mature, attaining to the whole measure of the fullness of Christ."

Philippians 2:1-4: "Therefore if there is any encouragement in Christ, if there is any consolation of love, if there is any fellowship of the Spirit, if any affection and compassion, make my joy complete by being of the same mind, maintaining the same love, united in spirit, intent on one purpose. Do nothing from selfishness or empty conceit, but with humility of mind regard one another as more important than yourselves; do not merely look out for your own personal interests, but also for the interests of others."

Colossians 3:14: "And over all these virtues put on love, which binds them all together in perfect unity."

These are just a few of the verses in the Bible that demand unity of the believers. If we are united, we are healthy. If we are healthy, we can grow. If you and I can believe that God wants our churches to be healthy, then perhaps we need to rethink our desire to walk away until we know that we've accomplished what we are supposed to and that God Himself is calling us away. Frustration in the ministry is normal. It is the most difficult of responsibilities in this life. All of us should have the goal of only exiting healthy churches.

You have this book in your hand because you want to do the right thing. Your patience has most likely worn thin and perhaps you wonder how you ever got into this mess in the first place. However, in the midst of your battle thoughts of staying or going, I plead with you, "Stay on in Ephesus" as long as you can and see what God can do.

Afterward:
Our Reward

Humans far too often work on the "rewards system." We like to have some recognition, some accolade, or even a prize for our successes. However, it is vitally important that ministers—especially those struggling in the ministry—realize that we have our reward already, and it's not heaven! Nor is it our salvation, or our family, or our calling, or our number of baptisms. Our reward is God.

In the Old Testament, the Levites were not given a portion of the land. God thought that they didn't need it. We see several times that God repeats Himself with the following statement, "But to the tribe of Levi, Moses did not give an inheritance, the Lord, the God of Israel, is their inheritance…" (Joshua 13:14, 33; Deuteronomy 18:1–2). This came from an earlier conversation between the lord and Aaron (Numbers 18:20). Although all believers are considered to be of the priestly line (1 Peter 2:9), the statement above should hold a special place in the heart of God's vocational and bivocational ministers, God *is* our reward. We work for the joy of being in His presence. Salvation, heaven, sanctification, and all of our great rewards are only avenues to give us the ultimate reward, the presence of God Himself.

Some of us will find great joy in the ministry; others will find hardship and difficulty at every turn. At times it will depend on us. In a different context, it may be due to struggles that existed before we were even born. However, we must remember that our greatest reward in ministry is to be in the presence of God. Our ministries must be defined by this truth. His presence is made possible for all of us through Christ. Our only real concern must not be fear of failure or losing face or disappointing others, but losing contact with His intimate presence. And, of course, we have His Word that this will never happen! (Hebrews 13:5).

With this perspective, it is more understandable why Paul put so much passion into Romans 8. We not only believe the promise of God to stick with us, but we can see that He was with us before the world was even created! Nothing can separate us from that. Therefore, we remain to this day, more than conquerors through Him who loves us! (Romans 8:37) "How great is the love that the father has lavished on us, that we shall be called the children of God!" (1 John 3:1). The next move is yours. Claim your reward! Utilize your inheritance! Seek to treasure Him even more!

Endnotes

1. Tony Kummer, April 21, 2007, comment on "How Old Are Most Southern Baptist Pastors?," *Said at Southern Blog*, April 21, 2007, http://saidatsouthern.com/how-old-are-most-southern-baptist-pastors/.
2. D. Scott Barfoot, Bruce E. Winston, Ph.D., and Charles Wickman,Ph.D.,"ForcedPastoralExits:AnExploratoryStudy." WorkingPaper.RegentUniversity,June2005.AccessedJuly2011. http://www.scottbarfoot.com/wp-content/uploads/2011/07/forced_pastoral_exits.pdf. Original research quoted J. C. LaRue, "Forced Exits: Preparation and Survival," *Christianity Today International/Your Church Magazine, July/August, 1996, 42 (4), 64.* Accessed December 27, 2002, from http://www.christianitytoday.com/cbg/features/report/6y4064.html.
3. "Forced Pastoral Exits: An Exploratory Study."
4. "Forced Pastoral Exits: An Exploratory Study."
    Only 45 percent of those who are forced to leave a ministry returned within the next year while churches who had forced a termination had employed a new minister within three months.
5. At times, the changing of a ministry position is based around preference including: change in calling, better

situation for family, general feeling that they have taken the church as far as they can, desire for a new town or church, desire to serve at a larger church, better pay/benefits. These preferences are commonly cited when the minister is asked about the motivation to resign. See Lisa Cannon Green, "Former Pastors Report Lack of Support Led to Abandoning Pastorate," accessed February 9, 2016, http://www.lifewayresearch.com/2016/01/12/former-pastors-report-lack-of-support-led-to-abandoning-pastorate/ Lisa Cannon Green, "Despite Stresses, Few Pastors Give Up on Ministry," accessed February 9, 2016, http://www.lifewayresearch.com/2015/09/01/despite-stresses-few-pastors-give-up-on-ministry/

6. Charles Willis, "Lifeway Executive Addresses Churches' 'Dirty Little Secret,'" *Baptist Press*, May 5, 1999, accessed February 9, 2016, http://www.bpnews.net/910.

7. Steve Hale Evangelistic Association, June 2, 2010 and Dr. Richard J. Krejcir, "Statistics on Pastors," accessed February 9, 2016, http://www.churchleadership.org/apps/articles/default.asp?articleid=42347&columnid=4545

8. Thom S. Rainer, *Breakout Churches: Discover How to Make the Leap* (Grand Rapids: Zondervan, 2005), 44–45. Here Rainer notes that less than one percent of surveyed ministers are "legacy leaders" who think of the future of the church beyond their own tenure.

9. R. Albert Mohler, Preface to Derek Prime and Alistair Begg, *On Being Pastor: Understanding our Calling and Work* (Chicago: Moody Publishers, 2004), 9.

10. Wayne E. Oates, *The Christian Pastor* 3rd ed. rev. (Philadelphia: Westminster Press, 1982), 9.

11. The two Greek terms, *presbyterous* and *episkopos*, used here interchangeably, are both translated as elder in this passage.

12. 12 ._John J. Polhill, *Acts: New American Commentary* (Nashville: Broadman and Holman, 1992), 425. Polhill notes that Paul makes himself the object lesson and the one to be emulated by other ministers.

13. Steve Walton, *Leadership and Lifestyle: The Portrait of Paul in the Miletus Speech and I Thessalonians* (Cambridge: Cambridge University Press, 2000), 17–18. Although the authorship of this Miletus Speech has been given Lucan authority by some (Bruce, 1943 and Hemer, 1989) Pauline authorship will be assumed, relying on both tradition and the strong ties between this letter and Paul's other epistles, especially Ephesians and 1 and 2 Timothy. See Ben Witherington III, *The Acts of the Apostles: A Socio-rhetorical Commentary* (Grand Rapids: Eerdmans, 1998), 610 for a chart comparing the themes of this speech with those in Paul's various epistles.

14. David J. Williams, *New International Biblical Commentary Acts* (Peabody: Hendrickson, 1990), 350.

15. Commentators consistently point to the goodbye as being in a league with—and the same form—as Jacob's in Genesis 29, Joshua's in Joshua 23–24 and Samuel's in 1 Samuel 12. See Ben Witherington III, *The Acts of the Apostles*, (Grand Rapids: Eerdmans, 1998), 612, for one example.

16. Robert G. Clouse, Richard V. Pierard and Edwin M. Yamauchi, *Two Kingdoms: The Church and Culture Through the Ages* (Chicago: Moody Press, 1993), 35. Many scholars believe that Paul worked as a tent maker in the morning and preached the Gospel in the afternoon. This would explain what is meant specifically by, "I worked among you."

17. Derek Prime and Alister Begg, *On Being Pastor* (U.S.A.: Prime and Begg), 50. The authors rightly note that all pastoral goals should be goals of stewardship only, since the possession of the congregation is Christ's alone.

18. D. Martyn Lloyd-Jones, *Spiritual Depression: Its Causes and Its Cure* (Grand Rapids: Eerdmans, 1998), 216.

19. This quote was used in the *Together for the Gospel* conference, where Mark Dever referenced a letter from John Brown—a Baptist pastor of considerable wisdom and experience—written to a newly ordained pastor who found himself entrusted with a church whose congregation was small in his own estimation.

20. Jesus demonstrated His anger when he cleansed the temple. Also, when the disciples rebuked the children before Christ held and blessed them.

21. Statistics taken from polling conducted by *Francis A. Schaeffer Institute of Church Leadership Development in a 2005 survey and verified by other reputable pollsters including Fuller Seminary, Focus on the Family and Barna.* See www.intothyword.org/apps/articles/default.asp?articleid=36562

22. Josh McDowell, *The New Evidence That Demands A Verdict Fully Updated To Answer The Questions Challenging Christians Today* (Nashville: Thomas Nelson, 1999), 2.
    D. Martyn Lloyd-Jones, *Preaching and Preachers* (Grand Rapids: Zondervan, 1971), 163. Lloyd-Jones adds, "… it is what is needed above all else."

23. Clyde Fant and William Pinson, introduction to "Biblical Sermons to Savonarola: ad 27–1498," in *A Treasury of Great Preaching, vol. 1.* (Dallas: Word, 1995), vii.

24. Charles H. Spurgeon, *Lectures to My Students* (Grand Rapids: Zondervan, 1979), 192–93.

25. Lloyd-Jones, *Preaching and Preachers*, 305. Lloyd-Jones then proceeds to give a biblical overview of the anointing, focusing especially on the Apostles. Using the promise of Acts 1:8, Lloyd-Jones states, "The significance, as I see it, is that here we have men whom, you would have thought, were in a perfect position and condition already to act as

preachers." Lloyd-Jones also speaks of the prophets, John the Baptist, Paul and Jesus as being examples of those anointed in their proclamation.

26. James Forbes, "The Holy Spirit and Preaching," *USA, Forbes, 1989, 83.*

27. Thomas C. Peters, *Simply C. S. Lewis: A Beginner's Guide to His Life and Works* (Wheaton: Crossway Books, 1997), 215.

28. When it comes to specific issues of conscience, like alcohol, the Roman principle of not making a brother stumble applies. Clearly, when it came to legal or allowable behavior, Paul told the Romans to abstain for the sake of unity.

29. John R. W. Stott, *The Preacher's Portrait* (Grand Rapids: William B. Eerdmans, 1961), 17.

30. Bryan Chapell, *Christ-Centered Preaching: Redeeming the Expository Sermon* (Grand Rapids: Baker Books, 1994)

    John Stott, *Between Two Worlds* (Grand Rapids: Eerdmans, 1982)

    Walter C. Kaiser, Jr., *Toward An Exegetical Theology* (Grand Rapids: Baker, 1981)

    Jerry Vines and Jim Shaddix, *Power in the Pulpit* (Chicago: Moody, 1999)

    Haddon W. Robinson, *Biblical Preaching* (Grand Rapids: Baker, 2001)

    Stephen F. Olford and David L. Olford, *Anointed Expository Preaching* (Nashville: Broadman & Holman, 1998)

31. Lloyd-Jones, *Preaching and Preachers*, 196.

32. Faris D. Whitesell, introduction to *Power in Expository Preaching* (Grand Rapids: Fleming H. Revell, 1963), viii.

33. Chapell, *Christ-Centered Preaching: Redeeming the Expository Sermon* 88.

34. Thom S. Rainer, *Effective Evangelistic Churches* (Nashville: Broadman and Holman, 1996) and Mark Dever, *9 Marks of a Healthy Church* (Wheaton: Crossway Books, 2004).

35. For a website full of charts and gathered statistics see the following website last accessed 2011, http://fastestgrowingreligion.com/numbers.html.

36. Robert D. Bergen, *1, 2 Samuel, The New American Commentary* (Nashville: Broadman and Holman, 1996), 412.

37. Research found by Greymatter Research and Consulting (formerly Ellison Research) in January 2009. 16 percent of Protestants were loyal to their denomination while 19 percent were loyal to a given brand of toilet paper and 22 percent to their chosen brand of toothpaste. http://www.greymatterresearch.com/index_Loyalt.htm.

38. See R. Kent and Barbara Hughes, *Liberating Your Ministry from the Success Syndrome* (Wheaton: Crossway, 2008) for a balanced discussion on ministerial priorities including work ethic,

39. Calvin Miller, *O Shepherd, Where Art Thou?* (Nashville: Broadman and Holman, 2006).

40. Richard Baxter, *The Reformed Pastor* 1656; repr. (Edinburgh: Banner of Truth Trust, 1954).

41. Irwin Raphael McManus, *An Unstoppable Force* (Loveland, Co: Group Press, 2001), 31.

42. Peter Gorday, ed., *Ancient Christian Commentary on Scripture, New Testament IX: Colossians, 1 and 2 Thessalonians, 1 and 2 Timothy, Philemon* (Downers Grove: InterVarsity Press, 2000) 130.

43. Gordon Fee, *New International Biblical Commentary: 1 and 2 Timothy* (Peabody: Hendrickson, 1984), 42.

44. First Timothy 4:16. Spurgeon refers to this act of the minister as "Self-watch." See C. H. Spurgeon, *Lectures to My Students* (Grand Rapids: Zondervan, 1996), 7.

45. C. H. Spurgeon, *Lectures to My Students*, 70.

46. Arthur W. Pink, *The Holy Spirit* (Grand Rapids: Baker Books, 1972), 43.

47. Thomas C. Oden, *Systematic Theology Volume Three: Life In the Spirit* (San Francisco: Harper Collins, 1992), 21.

48. MacArther, "Do Not Quench the Holy Spirit," accessed 2011, http://www.sermonaudio.com/sermoninfo.asp?sid=11612169390.

49. Mark A. Noll, *The Scandal of the Evangelical Mind* (Grand Rapids: William B. Eerdmans, 1994), 3. Noll's opening lines of this very profound and insightful book states, "The scandal of the Evangelical mind is that there is not much of an evangelical mind…American evangelicals are not exemplary for their thinking, and they have not been for several generations."

50. Merriam-Webster's online dictionary, accessed 2015, http://www.merriam-webster.com/dictionary/profound.

51. Carl F. H Henry et al., *Quest for Reality: Christianity and the Counter Culture* (Downers Grove: Intervarsity Press, 1973), 160.

www.ingramcontent.com/pod-product-compliance
Lightning Source LLC
Chambersburg PA
CBHW072138160426
43197CB00012B/2153